*A Con
Guia...
Investing, Minimizing Taxes
and Estate Planning*

So You Want More Money...

Here's What Works

GEORGE CANERS

B.Sc., C.A., M.B.A., C.F.P.

Peter
Good luck with your investments

George.
Feb 12/03

Marilyn Caners–Editor
Tom Janson–Producer
Fred Webster–Illustrator

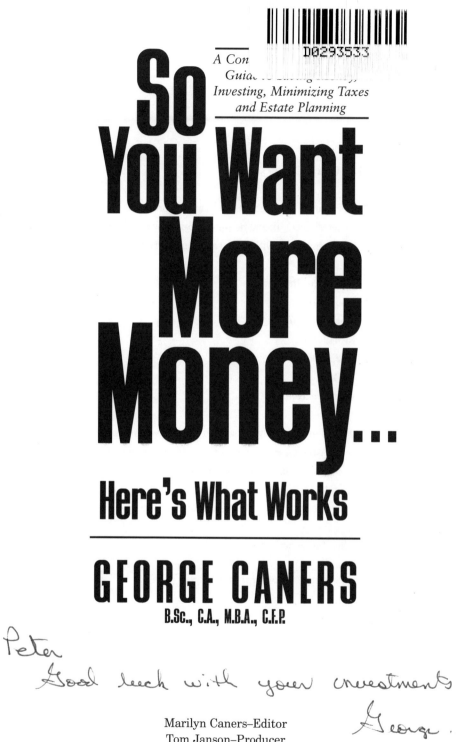

Published by Estate Services Inc.
 Suite 210, 9 Broad Street
 Brockville, Ontario K6V 6Z4
 Telephone: 613–342–1555
 Toll Free: 888–829–9952
 Fax: 613–342–2845
 e–mail: george@caners.com

Although the author has exhaustively researched all sources to ensure the accuracy and completeness of the information contained in this book, we assume no responsibility for errors, inaccuracies, omissions, or any inconsistency herein. Any slight of a person or an organization is unintentional. Readers should use their own judgement and/or consult a financial expert for specific applications to their individual situations.

First Edition published December 1998
Second Edition November 2001
CANADIAN CATALOGUING IN PUBLICATION DATA
Caners, George, 1948–
 So You Want More Money ... Here's What Works

ISBN 0–9684668–1–8
Finance, Personal. 2. Financial Security. I. Caners, Marilyn II. Title
HG179.C286 2001   332.024'01   C98–901443–6
Printed by: Performance Printing   (613) 283-5650
Cover Design: Digital Zone   (705) 748-5354
Text Design: Mejan Graphic Design   (613) 269-2821

SO YOU WANT MORE MONEY ...
Here's What Works

TABLE OF CONTENTS

ACKNOWLEDGEMENTS

I would like to begin by thanking my wife Marilyn, who is really the co–author as well as the editor of this book. Not having a financial background herself, she knew how important it was to produce a book that could be clearly understood by the average person. To this end, she worked tirelessly to translate my technical explanations into everyday language. She persisted in making me explain matters in more detail than I would have thought necessary. I appreciated her patience and dedication to our project.

The first edition was clearly a joint effort. Tom Janson did wonderful work in graph design, presentation, editing, and readying the manuscript for print. Fred Webster did a superb job of capturing the essence of what I was trying to say in his drawings. Tom, Fred, Marilyn and myself spent many long hours working together on the concepts and fine–tuning the final product. The book turned out to be far better than any of us could have accomplished alone. We fed on each other's ideas. Best of all, we had fun doing it.

Work on this second edition began almost as soon as the first edition was published. The concepts remain the same, but the information on how to implement them has been augmented.

A lot of insightful ideas and encouragement for both editions came from my three sons Chris, Jon and Kevin, my brother Dennis and his wife Debra, Arnold Berman, Don Grey, Suzanne Janson, Chris Punnett, Barry Raison, John Simpson, Brian Tuthill, and Jack Walker. There were times when I had doubts and was ready to quit before the first edition was completed. It was their support that kept me going.

Numerous others influenced me. First I wish to thank my parents. To this day, I marvel at how they raised 16 children on a small Manitoba farm. They were not rich, but through their ability to stretch a dollar, we always felt we had enough. They instilled in us their values of honesty, hard work and a belief that anything is possible. Their goal was to provide the opportunity for all their children to have a good formal education. This they accomplished well.

I am fortunate to have met some brilliant and honourable businessmen, especially David Beatty, Doug Hale, and Bob Lucey, from whom I learned a great deal. I am also grateful to my professors and the many financial authors who helped shape my thinking.

Finally, I wish to thank all my clients who shared with me their practical experiences. This book would not have been possible without them.

1

INTRODUCTION

I am an accountant with my own public practice. A major part of my work involves completing personal tax returns and doing financial planning. Over the years, I realized there was a common pattern in the methods used by people who had dramatically increased their wealth. By combining my financial knowledge with my clients' practical experiences, I developed my investment strat-

"How pleasant it is to have money!"

– Arthur Hugh Clough

(1819–1861)

egy. The result was that my own investments grew at a rate I thought was impossible. In retrospect, it was not by chance that this happened. The strategy was sound. The outcome was almost inevitable.

There is no doubt that the lack of personal financial security causes immense anxiety in many people. However, one wealthy man once said, "There is nothing easier than making money." This is a bit of an overstatement, but I understand what he is saying. So, if it is so easy to make money, why are so many people having such problems? How can such a contradiction exist? The answer lies in the way people approach saving and investing.

One experience in particular stimulated my curiosity about how wealth is created. I did financial work for two men who were employed by the same company. Both had university degrees, were married, had children, and were the same age. People would have assumed that they had comparable wealth. However, one had 100 times more money than the other! The reason? They had chosen different financial strategies.

There are three critically important elements required for financial success. The first of these is determination. People who are determined do not get discouraged when they have setbacks. They learn from them, try something different, and above all, they keep going. They know in the end that they will succeed. Can you imagine becoming a concert pianist if you are not determined to do so? Without a strong desire, you may learn how to play, but you will never perform at Carnegie Hall. Similarly, determination is the prerequisite for building financial freedom.

The second element is learning what you need to know to achieve your goal. To become a musician, you must learn how to read music and master the technique of playing your instrument. To get more money, you must know how to save and where to invest. The financial world is full of alluring traps. This book will provide you with the straightforward unbiased knowledge that you require.

The third element is follow-through. Nothing happens unless you take action. To become a concert pianist takes years of daily practice. To accumulate a lot of money takes years of daily saving. This is not easy, but when you see your money growing, you may be encouraged to stick with it. Begin your saving process as soon as possible. It is _never_ too late to start.

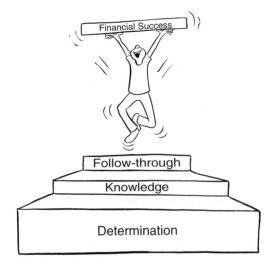

Increasing your wealth is analogous to growing trees. How much timber you end up with depends upon how many seedlings you plant and the length of time that they have to grow. Likewise, the more money you save and the longer you keep it invested, the more wealth you will accumulate. Saving is like planting seedlings.

Investment growth depends upon where you place your investments, just as much as tree growth depends upon where you plant your seedlings. A fertile environment is tremendously important.

At this point, I want to introduce you to a friend of mine, the "$6.50 a day man". He was always broke, but he decided to take control of his financial situation by saving $6.50 per day. Now, after a year of doing this, he has saved $2,373. (I will round this to $2,400 for simplicity.) By buying an RRSP and investing the resulting tax saving, he consequently has $4,000 to invest (this is explained in Chapter 6, "Registered Retirement Savings Plans"). His investment attains a rate of return of 12% (which is achievable if the advice in this book is followed). So, at the end of the first year he has $4,480.[1]

He plans to continue to save $6.50 per day and add the $4,000 annually to his investment. You can watch his progress. Each chapter will represent a year in his life; his accumulated savings to that point will be displayed in the box at the end of the chapter. You may be amazed at how well he does.

Years Invested	Total Savings
1	**$4,480**

---

[1] For simplicity, it is assumed that the savings are invested at the start of the year.

2

DRIFT, DROWN OR DECIDE

You are faced with three choices in financial planning, just as you are in other areas of life. You can drift, drown or decide.

The "drifter" floats aimlessly along on the huge ocean of life. The wind and the waves are the primary determinates of where he ends up. In spite of no plans, he eventually reaches the shore. A drifter feels life is not easy, but not bad either. The typical drifter lives in a house or condo. There is enough to get by on, but he cannot afford many luxuries. He doesn't understand finances very well. His retirement planning is minimal. It hardly occurs to him to put pen to paper, and figure it out ahead of time.

> "Nothing can stop the man with the right mental attitude from achieving his goal."
> – Thomas Jefferson

Drift

The "drowner" finds life a continuous struggle. It is not a matter of picking a shore to land on, but rather a case of managing to stay above the next wave as his boat is buffeted by gale force winds. He tires of trying to survive the many short–term crises that constantly arise. The drowner ends up in a small apartment, barely making ends meet. Life is tough, and he blames others for his misfortune. Retirement planning is non–existent.

Drown

The "decider" sees the shore and realizes that safety and the good life beckon her. The task becomes one of choosing which shore, and then where to land on that shore. She assesses her options, makes choices and acts on them. Abundance is there for the taking. The decider intuitively knows the easiest way to predict the future is to make it happen. She often puts pen to paper to see if she will have enough money to meet her needs. She has a lovely house at the edge of a lake.

Decide

I recently met a decider named Raghbir Dillon. He was the guest speaker at a stuttering refresher course that I was attending. His story literally kept me sitting on the edge of my chair. He spoke with amazing fluency and articulation, but he hadn't always. When he graduated as an engineer, he could not get a job in his field because of his speech impediment. He had such a severe stutter at that time that spoken communication was almost impossible for him. The only work that Raghbir could find was that of a draftsman.

His boss told him that to get ahead, he would have to learn to speak fluently. Raghbir attacked his problem with gusto, studying everything possible on the subject. He gave his boss a date on which he would do a presentation to his fellow employees. But as the date drew near, he was so fearful that he became ill. He could not do it.

Raghbir persisted in his quest for fluency. Finally, he learned about the Webster technique used by Dr. Robert Kroll at the Clark Institute in Toronto. This program gave him the tools he required to improve his speech and he practiced diligently. Raghbir joined Toastmasters to hone his speaking skills. He earned the title of "Distinguished Toastmaster" and frequently won awards at prestigious speaking contests.

Then life presented a new hurdle for him. He underwent major heart surgery. To regain his health, he took up exercise and now walks ten kilometres each day. He strongly advised us to do likewise.

Things were just getting under control when again tragedy struck. This time it was Parkinson's disease. In desperation he asked, "God why me?" But then he thought, "Am I not human? Do some humans not become ill? Then God, why not me?" He took up Tai Chi because he heard it would help. While doing research on the disease, he learned of a new surgical procedure that sounded promising. He became the 8th person in the world to undergo this operation to alleviate some Parkinson's symptoms. Now here he was helping us, instead of feeling like a victim.

Mahatma Gandhi also exemplified a decider. Once while he was boarding a moving train, one of his sandals fell off. He tried to reach back for it but it was too late. Then he took off his other sandal and threw it so that it landed beside the sandal he had dropped. Someone asked him why he had done that. Gandhi explained that one sandal was of no use to anybody.

This way at least one person would have a pair. He made the best of this situation, whereas many would have been upset.

I want to share a personal experience with you. All my life I have had a stutter. As a child I found it terribly humiliating. Twenty years ago, I attended a three–week intensive stuttering course that gave me the skills required to speak fluently. But it required rigorous daily practice. Soon I started to skip these practices and my stuttering returned. Seven months ago, I attended a weekend refresher course where I heard Raghbir's talk. He awakened my desire to speak fluently. Since that day, I have never missed a practice.

I now realize that there is a huge difference between wishing for something and truly wanting it. For example, Wayne Gretzky _really_ wanted to be a great hockey player. Do you have a strong desire to have more money? Are you willing to save with as much zeal as Wayne practiced his sport?

Years Invested	Total Savings
2	$9,498

3

THE BASICS

The reason we want more money is so that we can do whatever we want, whenever we want. Once you start saving and investing wisely, you'll discover the magic of compound interest: your money working for you all the time, even as you sleep. Over time your savings will earn more for you than you earn

> "Don't agonize.
>
> Organize."
>
> – Florynce Kennedy

from your job. At this point, you have achieved financial independence. You likely only have to save a small percentage of your income to make this happen. However, the saving must start as soon as possible, and must be continued until your goal is reached. It's like walking toward a destination. It is certain that you will get there, provided you keep moving in the right direction.

There are three steps to reach financial independence. First, determine what the goal is. How much money do you really want, and when do you want to have it? Next, establish a logical financial plan to reach this goal in the time provided. Finally, you must have a feedback system to monitor your progress. If your monitoring system indicates that you aren't achieving your goal, change your plan. A feedback system is meaningless if it does not encourage you to take action when warranted.

Determining your goal (being a decider) is by far the most important step in reaching financial independence. It is not enough to just think a goal is possible. You must know it is possible.

1. Your Goal

Most people require the money earned from a job to pay for their expenditures. The real purpose of wealth creation is to do away with the need to have a job. But this is only possible when the money you have saved generates enough cash to meet or exceed your expenditures. When you reach this point, work becomes a choice rather than a necessity. There is nothing that reduces work stress as much as the knowledge that you do not need the job.

Therefore, your goal becomes one of having sufficient savings to generate all the money that you require in order to do the things you want. Your plan will have an impact on how quickly you can accomplish this goal, and what lifestyle you can afford. Once you no longer need to work, and your retirement needs are taken care of, you may have further goals you want to reach. For example, you may wish to leave a legacy to your children, or fund a charitable cause to help those in need.

You must consider how long you can expect to live before you can calculate how much money you need for retirement. From 1970 to 1990, the life expectancy of the average Canadian at birth increased by five years.[2] Now the life expectancy is 78 years (the average of 75 for male and 81 for female). Your life expectancy actually increases as you age, because you have survived all the hazards that faced you from birth to that point in time. For example, as you reach adulthood, there is no longer a risk of dying from a childhood disease. At age 80, when you have given up skydiving and motorcar racing, your life expectancy is 87 if you are a male, and 89 if you are a female.

If you are now 30 years old, your life expectancy is 77 if you are male, and 82 if you are female. Assuming that you plan to retire at age 60, you will likely live for another 17 to 22 years after that, depending on your

---

[2] Statistics Canada (Tel: 888-297-7355)

gender. This is a long time to support yourself without the benefits of the cash inflow that a job provides. Make sure you have enough money saved prior to retiring.

How much money is enough? It depends on the person. Early on in my practice, a woman in her late 60's walked into my office and asked me to do her tax return, and her husband's. They had no investments whatsoever. Their only sources of income were the Canada Pension Plan (CPP) and Old Age Security (OAS). Their combined annual income was about $16,000. What I really found surprising was that they had given more than $2,000 to charity! I explained to her that because of their low income, they had no taxes to pay. Consequently their charitable receipts would provide them with no taxable benefit. She didn't care. There was a warm glow about this lady. She felt extremely lucky that they could give $2,000 to help others. They had no savings, and yet they appeared to have no need for any. This couple was able to live comfortably on less than their $16,000 income. I will never forget this remarkable woman. She was the "richest" person I had ever met because she felt abundance. This feeling is the only true measure of wealth. It has nothing to do with how much money you have in the bank.

On the other side of the spectrum is another client I greatly respect. Before retiring, he believes he should own his house outright, and have at least $3 million in liquid assets (money in the bank, GICs, shares and bonds). One million is to provide an income stream, one million is to buy toys he so desires, and the third million is his safety net. He has achieved this, and is still working to accumulate more wealth. Most would consider his requirements excessive. You are likely to find your capital needs somewhere between these two extremes of zero and $3 million.

To answer the question of how much money you need to "retire" (meaning work is not necessary for income), try the three–quarters rule. Retired people spend about three–quarters of what they used to spend when they were working. Calculate what you are spending now i.e. what you earn less what you save. Take three–quarters of that amount, and make adjustments for changes in your lifestyle. For example, if you plan to travel extensively during your retirement, you may need more money than you did while working. On the other hand, if you prefer to sit back and take it easy, then your requirements will be much less than when you were working. Therefore, it is important for you to first determine what your plans are before applying the three–quarters rule.

Your Goal

There is another fact to consider. Many of the basic necessities of life, e.g. apples, oranges, tissue, soap, etc., cost the same to all people, whether they are rich or poor. Someone at a lower–income level may require more than three–quarters of pre–retirement income to buy these necessities. Someone with a higher income would require less than three–quarters to do the same. For example, someone earning $20,000 while working may have difficulty living on $15,000 (75% of $20,000). However, someone earning $60,000 while working would probably require less than $45,000 (75% of $60,000).

Remember that so far all you have calculated is the amount of money you need. Let's look at how much savings you must have to generate enough income for retirement. Over the past 50 years (1950 – 2000), savings invested in five–year term deposits have provided an average rate of return (interest earned) of 8%.[3] At this rate, each $100,000 of savings would produce $8,000 of annual revenue. You could also spend some of this $100,000, but you would then be left with less money to generate future income, so be careful. Now you can see why you need to start sav-

---

[3] The actual rate of return was 7.7%; 2000 Andex Chart for Canadian Investors, Andex Associates Inc. (Tel: 800–524–2781)

ing early. It takes a lot of money to generate enough wealth to live comfortably. To determine how much investment is required to support expenses, I use a much more sophisticated calculation for my clients. It considers the rate of return expected from their savings, when they plan to stop working, inflation, and taxes. However, the three-quarters rule is much easier to understand and puts you in the ballpark.

One investor friend of mine feels you shouldn't even count on earning 8% annually. He believes you should only expect an annual rate of return of 5% to 7%. In other words, you would need savings of $114,000 to $160,000 to generate $8,000 annually. An easier way of remembering this is that you would need to save 15 to 20 times more than the amount of income you want generated.

One of the realities of life is inflation. It averaged 4.2% per year over the past 50 years.[4] At this rate, your money loses half of its value every 17 years. Therefore, every $1,000 of savings at retirement (age 50) will be worth only $500 at age 67, and only $250 at age 84.

After you have determined the amount of income you wish to have, the next step is to calculate how much you can expect from all sources other than investments. For example, will you receive money from the Canada Pension Plan? If so, how much? Your CPP pension income will vary depending on how much you paid into it while you were working, and on whether or not you decide to start drawing it prior to turning 65.

You should already receive an annual CPP Statement of Earnings. It tells you what you can expect to receive from CPP when you turn 65, based on what you have paid in to date. To ascertain how much your future income will add to your CPP benefit, contact Human Resources Development Canada at 1–800–277–9914. They will be happy to help you calculate this.

You may start to draw CPP as early as age 60, but only if you no longer work. However, for every month you draw it prior to your turning 65, your pension payout will permanently decrease by 0.5%. In other words, if you start to draw CPP five years early, your pension will be low-

---

[4] 2000 Andex Chart for Canadian Investors, Andex Associates Inc.

ered by 30% (60 months times 0.5%) for as long as you collect it. In spite of this, it is not a bad idea to take your CPP as soon as possible, as demonstrated in the following table. By drawing it at age 60, you have received $42,000 before the person who waits until 65 even starts. It is true that after you reach the age of 76, you will not have received as much pension as someone who decided to start collecting at age 65, but assuming the early payouts were invested, you will still be money ahead.

CPP Age 60 versus Age 65			
Period pension collected	Drawing CPP at age 60 Assume $700/month (70% Payout)	Drawing CPP at age 65 Assume $1,000/month	Total difference to date (By drawing CPP at age 60 vs. 65)
Age 60–65	$42,000	$0	$42,000
Age 65–70	$42,000	$60,000	$24,000
Age 70–75	$42,000	$60,000	$ 6,000
Age 75–80	$42,000	$60,000	($12,000)

You must contribute to CPP if you are still working past age 65; however, if you retire and start to draw CPP, you are exempt from making further payments into it should you go back to work.

If you retired in 2000, the maximum annual payment that you can receive from CPP is $9,155. Thereafter, payments may be adjusted slightly each year to compensate for inflation.

Another source of income for some people is Old Age Security (for 2000, the annual maximum was $5,080). OAS payments commence only after you turn 65. The factors influencing the amount received are rather complex, as they depend upon how long you were a resident of Canada, and how much income you currently earn. This is further explained in the Claw Backs section of Chapter 16, "Income Taxes". To find out more about the amount of income you can expect from OAS, call 1–800–277–9914 (the same number as for CPP information).

You may also have a company pension plan. It is very possible that with a generous pension plan, you will be able to enjoy a good retirement without the need for any other savings. If you don't have a pension, you must rely on your own Registered Retirement Savings Plan (RRSP) and other savings. (RRSPs are covered in detail in Chapter 6.) Let's look at the statistics. Only 33% of the Canadian labour force has a company pension plan.[5] Some plans, such as teachers' pension plans, have high premiums (what employees pay in), and provide a handsome pay-off, which is indexed to inflation. Another example of a generous pension plan is the one paid to federal and provincial politicians. Far behind, but still excellent, are civil servant and public sector pension plans. Very few private sector plans are as good. The reason is obvious. These plans are a significant cost to the employer, whose first goal is to protect the bottom line and make a dollar.

Canadians can contribute up to 18% of their previous year's earned income to an RRSP up to an annual maximum of $13,500. Canada Customs and Revenue Agency (formerly Revenue Canada) has a specific definition for earned income. For most people, earned income is the amount made from employment. Someone who always invests the maximum allowed in RRSPs, and works to age 65, will likely not have a shortage of money during retirement. What is your situation?

If you do have a company pension plan, it reduces the amount you are allowed to tax shelter (defer from tax) in an RRSP. Don't worry about this. Your employer has put money aside for you in a pension plan, and that is why your RRSP limit has been reduced. The combined company pension, plus the amount you put away in an RRSP, should provide the same tax benefit as if you contributed the entire amount to an RRSP. If you are not using all of your RRSP "room" (the cumulative total of yearly contributions that you are allowed to make), your savings goal may be too low. Start rectifying the situation now by filling up the unused RRSP room. Buying RRSPs and paying down debt are the two best strategies to provide you with more money in the future.

---

[5] Statistics Canada, Pension Plans in Canada, Report Number 74–401, Table 4.

Company pensions are often based on an employee's five highest–paid years. Suppose that in your five final years of work you earned $36,000, $37,000, $38,000, $39,000, and $40,000 respectively. Your average income for these years was $38,000. Now assume that the payout from this pension is 70%. Your actual pension payment will be 70% of $38,000 or $26,600 annually. Most pension plans allow you to elect a continuity option when you retire. This option decreases your payments while you are still alive, but continues to pay your spouse when you die. In this example, you could lower your pension payout to 60% of $26,600 or $15,960 annually. Your spouse would continue to receive this same amount should you die.

Upon death, all pension payments will cease if the continuity option was not chosen when the pension was set up. On the other hand, RRSPs do not vanish with the death of the person who holds them. The balance is passed tax–free to the spouse, providing that he/she is the beneficiary and the money is transferred directly to his/her RRSP. If there is no spouse, or if the RRSP funds are willed to someone else, then at death this tax–sheltered money is brought into income, taxes are paid on it, and the balance is given to the estate.

An annual pension of $15,960 may appear adequate to you, but with 4.2% inflation, this pension will only be worth about $8,000 in 17 years and $4,000 in 34 years. Perhaps you will require savings, as well as your pension, to support your lifestyle. Err on the side of caution. Start saving now. I have yet to hear a single person complain because he or she has saved too much. As already discussed, a significant portion of your life may be spent in retirement. It makes good sense to begin preparing early for what will hopefully be a long and healthy life.

Right now, get a pen and a piece of paper. How much more money do you need to save before you have the option of retiring? How many years will it take to get there at your current savings rate? Are you happy with this? What, if anything, are you going to do about it? Don't start reading again until you have calculated how much you need to retire in the lifestyle of your choice. Remember, it is better to be vaguely right than not knowing at all.

2. Your Financial Plan

You now know how much money you want. You also know what to expect as income from CPP, OAS, and pension plans. Income generated from your investments must make up any shortfall.

This is where your financial plan comes into play. Start by saving $6.50 per day. In a year you will accumulate $2,373, which rounds to $2,400. To grow these savings, put them into an RRSP. Your $2,400 will immediately become $4,000 because of tax savings. (This is discussed at length in Chapter 6, "Registered Retirement Savings Plans".) The following graph shows the results of annually contributing $4,000 to an RRSP. It is assumed that this money is invested and earns a 12% rate of return. Note that after only ten years of contributions, the investment already has a value of $78,618.

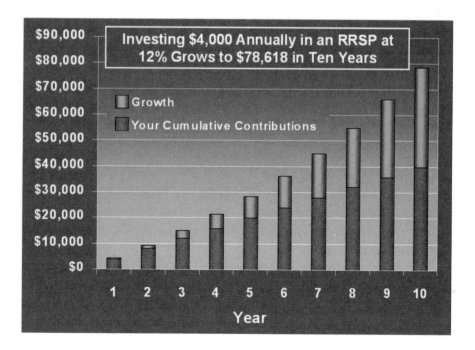

The 12% rate of return used in the calculation is attainable if you follow the strategy that is outlined later in this book. During the past 50

years (1950–2000), Canadian shares on average earned 11.5%. American shares have done even better, earning an average of 14% per year for the same period.[6] To focus on a more recent time frame, for the past ten years (1991–2000) Canadian shares averaged 13% and U.S. shares averaged 18%.[7]

You may be surprised to know that in 1998, only 29% of Canadian taxpayers contributed to an RRSP. Their median contribution was $2,500.[8]

3. Your Feedback System

A feedback system monitors how your financial plan is working. It gives you accurate information on where you are spending, how much you are saving and how your investments are doing.

Using Accurate Information

Occasionally my father used to play poker with his friends. It always amused him that when the players around the table at evening's end shared how well they had done, the total money won was always greater than the total money lost, even though these amounts should have been the same. My dad didn't think anyone lied deliberately, but he was convinced that the winners generally kept accurate score while the losers didn't.

Many people think they have done well on the stock market when that is not the case. They remember their gains and forget some of their losses. Or they think they have done well because their investments are up by 10%, even though the whole market has gone up 15%. They are really 5% behind where they should be.

People who buy lottery tickets, play a lot of bingo, or frequently visit casinos, usually do not have an accurate feedback system. If they did have one, I think they would be discouraged from gambling (assuming that they were not suffering from an addiction to it). Without correct information, we are in the same position as our ancestors who believed that the

---

[6] 2000 Andex Chart for Canadian Investors, Andex Associates Inc. (Tel: 800–524–2781).
[7] The Globe and Mail.
[8] Statistics Canada, Small Areas and Administrative Data Division, "1998 RRSP Contributors".

earth was the centre of the universe. It took the calculations of Polish astronomer Copernicus to help us understand that the planets revolved around the sun.

An effective feedback system is absolutely essential as a basis for making logical investment decisions.

Getting Organized

Getting organized is essential to developing a good feedback system. Start by having all your financial records in only one place so that they can be retrieved easily. To do this, purchase a two–drawer filing cabinet. One drawer is for your permanent files – those items that you are finished with, but want to keep. Examples of these include your old bank statements, tax returns with attached receipts, contracts, and legal documents. Make sure that each document is filed in a properly labelled envelope so that it cannot get lost.

The other drawer is used for more current documents. Examples of these include recent bank statements, utility bills, and statements for credit cards and investments. In this drawer, my wife and I also have a big envelope marked "Taxes" in which we put all receipts required to file next year's tax return e.g. RRSPs, charitable donations, T–4 and T–5 slips, tuition receipts and medical expenses. This system works well for us. We can put our hands on any of this information in a matter of minutes.

Cash

I never knew where I spent my money until I started to use the tracking system that my university roommate taught me. He would start each week by recording (in a small notebook) the amount of paper money in his wallet. Each evening he would record only the paper money spent during the day, and ignore all coin. For instance, if he bought a cup of coffee for $1.50 with a $10 bill, he would get back a $5 bill and $3.50 in change. Five dollars of paper money would now be gone. This would therefore be recorded as "coffee... $5.00", and would be subtracted from his starting amount. If later in the day, he bought another coffee and this time spent only change on it, he would not record it. At the end of the week, he would compare what paper money he had left in his wallet to the amount left according to his notebook. If the two figures didn't agree, it either meant he forgot to record something, or he had lost some money.

I use my roommate's system to this day. The notebook is kept in my top desk drawer at work. It takes me only a few minutes, a couple of times a week, to record where money was spent. Once a month, I take five minutes to total the expenditures, accounting for which of my out–of–pocket expenses relate to my business. It's the type of workload I can handle.

Banking

My wife and I have just one joint chequing account, which forms the heart of our feedback system. Marilyn maintains a running bank balance by recording all deposits to, or withdrawals from, this account. To do this she carries a chequebook in her purse. Not only does she record withdrawals such as cheques written, she also records each time she uses her debit card. Therefore, we always know how much money is in the bank. (By the way, Canada is a world leader in the use of debit cards.)

We put all recurring bills, such as Ontario Hydro, on automatic bank debit. My job is reduced to just updating the chequebook record when notices of these bills arrive.

We usually try to pay non– recurring bills as soon as we receive them. This is done for several reasons. First, we hate owing money. Second, the bill is handled and out of the way. Third, the local people that we deal with appreciate quick payment. Finally, when our bank account goes down, we are less tempted to spend money.

When we receive our bank statement, I do a bank reconciliation i.e. compare it to Marilyn's chequebook record. For every transaction that I confirm on the bank statement and then tick off, I also tick it off in the chequebook. I then add up the cheques that have been written, but haven't yet cleared the bank (i.e. the ones in the chequebook with no ticks beside them). I round off the cents to the next highest dollar. I subtract this amount from the closing balance on the bank statement. This balance is what the running bank balance should be in our chequebook record. If the chequebook record is in error, it is adjusted to what the correct balance should be. Doing a bank reconciliation also verifies that all the transactions on the account are indeed ours and not someone else's.

Many people spend a lot of time finding where they have made an addition and/or subtraction error in their own chequebook record. I don't. I trust the bank's computers to accurately do this task for me. My bank reconciliation never takes me more than 15 minutes. It pays to keep things simple, because then they get done.

I knew one couple that had six bank accounts: hers, his, joint, rent, insurance, and savings. They were always transferring money from one account to another to cover cash shortfalls. All this complexity did not add to their wealth ... it just added to their work. It is much easier to juggle just one ball than to juggle many. Similarly, the key to a good feedback system is to keep it simple, so that attention will be focused on important matters.

Credit Cards

I have only one credit card and I use it for most of my purchases. I do this because it is handy, and it provides me with a record of what I bought. The credit card statement becomes my feedback system.

Every time the credit card is used, the receipt goes in my wallet. Once or twice a week, I record the amounts in a notebook, keeping a running total of what I owe. The receipts are put in an envelope, and I keep this and the notebook in my top desk drawer at work. Each month is kept in a separate envelope, marked accordingly. This system takes very little time, and provides valuable information. It tracks what I am spending my money on, and gives me a record to check against my credit card statement. I know my outstanding credit card balance at any time. If need be, I can verify this amount by calling the credit card company. This knowledge puts me in charge. Because I am always aware of every expenditure I make and how much I owe, I'm less likely to buy frivolously. It helps me put the brakes on spending and fuels my saving.

Modern technology gives you another way to track your credit card spending. You can use the Internet to see what expenditures have gone through, and to check your current balance. (You can also use the Internet to check on your bank account or loan balances, pay bills, transfer money and place investments.) If interested, check how to do this with your bank. For those who are computer-minded, the Internet provides excellent and up to date feedback.

It is not necessary to have more than one credit card, although many people have more. A credit counsellor once told me that a client of his had thirty–eight credit cards! Did you realize that was even possible? There are no rewards for complexity. It is likely that this consumer had no idea of his outstanding credit card balances.

It is a good idea, however, for a husband and wife to have separate credit and debit cards from each other. But it is not enough just to have your own credit card. You must ensure that your card is not linked to that of your spouse i.e. you must be the "primary" credit card holder and not the "joint applicant" with your spouse. One disadvantage of being a "joint applicant" is that your credit card may be cancelled if your spouse dies.

Banks report your credit card payments to the credit bureau on a monthly basis. The bureau relies heavily on this information to determine your ability to handle credit responsibly. Make sure you are never late with the required payment. Having a good credit rating will help you to get a bank loan more easily.

There is another reason why Marilyn and I have separate credit cards. Once when we were at a restaurant in San Francisco, my credit card wouldn't work. Fortunately, hers did.

Investments

My wife and I each have one self–administered RRSP account. Also, we jointly have just one investment account at a discount brokerage house (a corporation that specializes in buying and selling shares and bonds). This means that between the two of us we receive just one T–5 slip, which is the tax slip reporting interest and dividend income. Note how simple this makes our tax returns.

The investments within our RRSPs and joint investment account are solely in shares of blue chip corporations. I buy more when I have spare cash. I rarely sell. My goal is to accumulate wealth.

At the end of each month, my broker sends me my account statement, which notes the number of shares held, their market value (what they are worth), as well as any money not yet invested. When I receive this statement, I verify that the number of shares and amount of cash are correct. Usually, there is no change from the previous month, so this takes no time at all. I keep these statements in a three–ring binder.

I use an easy method to ascertain how my investments are doing from month to month. On January 1ˢᵗ of each year, I record in the binder the value of my investments from the December statement. During the year I make a note of any money added to or withdrawn from the account. Let's assume that the December value of all my investments and cash in the account was $50,000. I refer to this as my base amount. I compare this figure to what my investments are worth at any time during the year. For example, if at the end of February my statement shows a value of $52,000, I know that my investments have gone up $2,000 or 4% ($2,000 divided by

$50,000).[9] Now assume that in April I add $5,000 to my base amount of $50,000 to give a new base amount of $55,000. If my statement at the end of April shows a total value of $60,000, I know that since the start of the year my investments have gone up $5,000 or 9% ($5,000 divided by $55,000). I like to compare my rate of return to the market average, such as the S&P 500 Index that is explained later.

I summarize performance on a yearly basis, and decide if I should make any changes. The question that I always ask myself is why not sell my least favourite investment and buy more of the one that I like the most?

Many people use their computer to keep track of their investments. Be mindful that if you are dependent on your computer for feedback, it may be an indication that your investments are too complicated.

The Internet is a wonderful tool to use in checking the current value of your shares. Don't be enticed to trade by watching the daily share value rise and fall. Remember that your investments are long term.

Is Your Feedback System Working? If Not, Take Action

To check if your feedback system is working, see if you can answer the following questions. Do you know how much money is in your wallet right now? About how much money is in your bank account? Do you keep your bank machine withdrawal slips until you have updated your bank records? What is the up–to–date outstanding balance on your credit card? In other words, what would you owe if you were to pay off your credit card in full today? Finally, do you know the total balance of your investments as of the end of last month? If you are unsure of the above amounts, or cannot get these numbers quickly from your own records, you need to modify your feedback system.

It has been my experience that people with no financial worries can easily answer the preceding questions. They are careful with money. They know where they spend it. With accurate feedback, they can draw valid conclusions and constantly fine-tune their strategy. On the other hand,

---

[9] To obtain the percentage, the bracketed number must be multiplied by 100.

people with money problems often feel they are not in control. Their feed-back system ranges from poor to non-existent. They spend without being fully aware of how they stand financially. It is no accident that those with a poor feedback system tend to have the least wealth.

Years Invested	Total Savings
3	$15,117

4

SAVE BEFORE SPENDING

The prerequisite for saving is learning to spend less than you earn. This action will free up some money, which will grow rapidly if invested wisely. The amount saved, plus its growth, must be sufficient to meet your future monetary needs.

The following point may encourage you to save. Let's suppose your employer gives you a $2,000 raise. After taxes are paid on it, you would be left with about $1,000. Another way

> "If your outgo exceeds your income, then your upkeep will be your downfall."
>
> – Bill Earle

to have an extra $1,000 would be to cut back on your expenditures by the same amount. Therefore, every time you manage to save some money, imagine that your boss just gave you a pay raise of twice that amount.

My father was very frugal when it came to spending money. One of his favourite expressions was, "You can't save water in a leaky bucket." The first illustration shows how this saying can be applied to saving money. Water coming into the savings bucket represents income and the leaks represent spending. Unless the inflow exceeds the outflow, you will be left with no savings. Therefore, job number one is to patch the holes in your savings bucket so that it can hold water.

Savings Bucket

Spending Money

Let's examine how you spend your money. The three categories consist of an expense, a depreciating asset, and an appreciating asset:

1. An expense is an item or activity where, once the money is paid out, it is gone. None of it can be recaptured. A large portion of your money goes towards expenses, which include things such as living costs, entertainment, holidays and dining out.

2. A depreciating asset loses value over time. The longer it is held, the less valuable the item becomes. Examples include your car, furniture, computer, and stereo system.

3. An appreciating asset is something that is expected to increase in value as time passes. Examples include shares and bonds.

It is important to note that if you want your wealth to grow, you have to spend less on expenses, and more on appreciating assets. You must realize that you have these choices.

Most people feel that the more assets they have (car, boat, cottage) the richer they are. My friend believes that all these things actually make you poorer as they consume cash. For instance, purchasing a cottage will most likely trigger related expenses such as furniture, decorating, landscaping and repairs. To become wealthy, he feels we must reverse our thinking about what constitutes an asset.

Before buying an expensive item such as a motor home, cottage, time-share, ski–doo, or boat, you may want to consider renting it for a while first. If your initial enthusiasm for the item wanes, you simply stop renting.

One of the cardinal rules of financial planning is that it is never wise to borrow money for an expense. Instead, save for it. When you incur that expense e.g. a dream vacation, you will really enjoy it because you have looked forward to it and it is pre–paid. Be in control. Financial pressure causes a great deal of stress to many people. By saving before spending, a lot of financial worries can be alleviated.

Credit cards are handy to use, but be aware that they do encourage you to spend more. Local merchants tell me that there is no doubt that their customers are not as price sensitive when they use a credit card instead of cash. The convenience of plastic makes impulse buying much easier.

A credit card company earns a lot of money by collecting fees from the merchants (up to 4% of their credit card sales). But it earns the bulk of its money from the interest charged to the credit card holders when they do not pay off their monthly balance. The more consumers use credit cards, the more credit card companies make. Therefore, they offer incentives to encourage use of their card. One example of such an incentive is air miles. For every dollar you spend with your card, you receive one air mile. It requires 15,000 air miles to fly from Toronto to Winnipeg. If you book early, this trip costs about $480.[10] Spending $15,000 to get a flight worth $480 is not a huge reward.

Over 60% of Canadians do not pay off the full balance on their credit cards every month.[11] This usually indicates that these folks are having financial problems because their expenses exceed their income. They add to their dilemma by having to pay costly credit card interest, which is commonly 16 to 18 %. Many people don't realize that if the monthly balance is not paid off, interest is charged from the date the item was purchased instead of from the date the credit card payment is due, which is often a month later.

If you pay interest on your credit cards, strong action must be taken to stop this leak in your savings bucket. Perhaps the card should be cut up. Another solution that one couple had was to freeze their credit card in a block of ice. Apparently, the only way to get at the card without wrecking it was to let the ice melt, allowing them to seriously rethink their spending. This measure worked for them.

---

[10] Air Canada quote October 2000.
[11] Royal Bank Visa Centre, October 1998.

It is no small feat to bring your spending under control. Change the habit of using your credit card to one of using cash or a debit card instead. Stephen Covey claims it takes only 21 days to create a new habit.[12] This is not a long time to learn to save before spending.

In general, there is a pattern in how much you spend and save at various stages of your life.[13] There are two phases when spending is high. The first one occurs concurrently with the purchase of your first house and the birth of your children. The second phase is when the children leave home to start post–secondary education. In–between these phases, you will be able to contribute the most to your savings.

Save Before Spending

Regardless of the stage you are in, saving some money is very important. Remember, it is akin to cultivating a forest. If you fail to plant seedlings, there will never be trees to harvest. This point cannot be overemphasized. There is no magic. The only way to acquire seedlings in the first place is to follow the "save before spending" rule. You must resist the lure of advertising that encourages you to spend every cent you make. Instead, choose to save a portion from each paycheque, and then spend the rest only as required. This approach is often referred to as "paying yourself first".

One method to save before spending is to make arrangements with your employer for a pre–authorized payroll deduction, whereby a predetermined amount of money is deducted from your cheque, and deposited directly into your investment account. On the other hand, you may have already arranged for your entire paycheque to be automatically deposited into your chequing account. In that case, you can ask your banker or stockbroker to regularly withdraw money from that account, for deposit into an investment account. Your nest egg will be accumulating without you even lifting a finger. Many people find they do not miss money that they have never seen in the first place.

Consider the following two individuals. One man has no investments put aside for his future, but is overflowing with ideas of how to save

---

[12] "The 7 Habits of Highly Effective People", Stephen R. Covey.
[13] "Boom, Bust and Echo, How to Profit from the Coming Demographic Shift", David F. Foote with Daniel Stoffman.

money by finding good deals. The problem is that all his "saving" involves spending more money. The other man always has more income tax deducted from his paycheque than is necessary, so at tax time he receives a sizable refund. Every year this refund is used to buy next year's RRSPs. He has learned to save before spending. Granted, he is not earning any interest on the money he is lending to the tax department. However, even though the method may not be perfect, at least it guarantees that money is saved.

Some people find that budgeting really helps them save. Others, including myself, simply hate budgeting. If you can budget effectively, by all means do it. If you can't, don't feel guilty.

How do I personally save before spending? I invest the maximum allowable in RRSPs, and do so as soon as I can. In other words, I buy my RRSPs on January 2nd of the year to which the tax savings will apply, instead of waiting for the final deadline of February 28th of the next year. I feel committed to doing this, so I save all year for it. If I don't have all the money by January 2nd, I still buy all my RRSPs by borrowing the balance. I pay off this loan as soon as possible.

When I can manage it, I put any extra cash I have into investments outside my RRSPs. Once the money is invested, I am steadfast in keeping it there. If I need money to cover an unexpected cash flow problem, I would sooner take out a short–term loan than cash in these investments. This saving system is not fancy, but it works for me. Does your system work for you?

John Templeton is one of the great investors of our time. He is a firm advocate of the "save before spending" principle. In his autobiography, he mentions that he and his wife worked hard to save half of what they earned! This process began as soon as they were married. Because they started to save a lot of money early, is it any wonder that John Templeton and his wife became very wealthy? Using the analogy of tree planting, it is obvious that Mr. Templeton recognized the value of planting a huge number of seedlings as soon as he could. He also had the wisdom to plant them in places where they grew quickly into large trees.

Summary

The final word about saving goes to Dr. Steven F. Venti of Dartmouth College in Hanover, New Hampshire and Dr. David A. Wise of Harvard University.[14] These professors did extensive scientific research to determine why people had a wide range of accumulated wealth as they approached retirement. They found that it did not depend upon the amount of money earned during the respondents' working lives. Many people with low incomes retired wealthy and many people with high incomes retired broke. It did not depend upon the type of investments made e.g. aggressive, risky or safe. Nor did luck play a role. *The difference in retirement wealth was due to the amount people decided to save during their working years.*

Almost three–fourths of the respondents realized that they had saved too little. The fact that so many of these were high–income earners was in the researchers' words, "striking". The professors found that those who had a plan tended to retire with more wealth than those who did not. The most effective plan was to set aside something from each paycheque.

Years Invested	Total Savings
4	$21,411

---

[14] "Choice, Chance, and Wealth Dispersion at Retirement", National Bureau of Economic Research, Working Paper 7521 "Income".

5

EXAMINE YOUR NEEDS

The goal of business is to create such strong needs in us that we are willing to part with our money. It has worked. Society's desire for more appears insatiable. In the past decade, the average size of an American home has increased by 46%. The number of cars per American adult has risen 100%; the average is now one car per person over 16. There are 220% more amusement parks. The number of people taking cruises has increased 1200%. In spite of all this spending, it is not leading us to more happiness.[15] After one need is fulfilled, it is not long before we again feel empty. The process is never–ending, similar to a dog chasing its own tail.

> "The richest man, whatever his lot, is he who is content with what he has got."
> – Dutch Proverb

Limiting your needs will help you to save. The more you want "things", the more control you must exert to stop yourself from buying too much. Do whatever it takes. After a while, the growth from your investments will exceed your monetary needs. At this point, you no longer have to restrain yourself from spending.

---

[15] "Money Can Get You Toys...But Are You Happy?", Kathy Bergen, The Financial Post, Sept 9, 2000.

A friend of mine is skilful at avoiding marketing ploys. A few years ago, he and I were with a group of 40 other men on a two–day ski trip to Mount Tremblant, Quebec. A major ski manufacturer was offering free product trials for their new "carving skis". These skis are supposed to help a good skier look like an expert. I asked my buddy if he was going to take the company up on its offer. "No," he said. I was surprised because he is a pretty good skier, and I thought he would be interested in testing these new skis, especially since there was no cost involved.

He then explained his rationale. He was not in the market for new skis. If he tried the new skis and found he did not like them, he had just wasted a bit of time. On the other hand, if the new skis were a little better than his current ones, all he accomplished was to create a need that currently didn't exist. He pointed out that he was happy with his present equipment.

I know others who make conscious decisions to avoid spending. One fellow in Montreal says it is easier for him to save if he is not near the stores. He finds a walk in the park much more enjoyable, and much less costly, than a walk through a mall. Another avoids reading newspapers and watching TV. He sees these media instruments as platforms for advertisers to stimulate a need in him. He feels that if he doesn't see the ads, he won't be tempted to spend.

How do you know how much you are spending in relation to others around you? Some people believe that the amount of garbage you put out each week is an accurate measure of your consumption. It is also an indication of the amount of pre–packaged goods you buy. Bulk buying is cheaper and produces less garbage.

Some people seem naturally frugal. I recall a neighbour from my childhood in rural Manitoba. This man would paint his farm truck once every ten years. We would try to calculate the vehicle's age by remembering how many times it had changed colour. Yes, he may have been a tad too thrifty, but he certainly could teach us a lot about not wasting too much money on our vehicles. Another person I remember is Mr. Kubas, my grade two teacher. He had one pink eraser, which at that time had already lasted him for five years. He tried to develop the same "careful not to waste" habits in his students.

Of course, there are people on the other side of the spectrum. One person I know, with a negative net–worth (i.e. more debts than assets), traded in her one–year–old car for the latest model. When I asked her why she had done that, she said she liked the look of the dash on the new car slightly better. She had no idea how much extra this cost her, but thought that she would be able to make the payments.

A lot of the money we earn goes toward paying for the need to have a car. There are two types of costs involved – ownership costs and operating costs.

Ownership costs include things such as depreciation (the difference between what you paid for the car and its current value), insurance, licence and registration, and finance expense. These costs tend to be fixed i.e. they do not change with the amount that you drive. You are locked into ownership costs the moment you make the purchase.

The type of car you buy will determine the ownership costs. If you want to reduce them, then consider purchasing a less expensive vehicle and do without costly options such as a sunroof, all wheel drive, or heated seats.

Following is the breakdown of the ownership costs of a 2000 Chevrolet Cavalier LS four–door sedan with a 2.2 litre, 4–cylinder engine. The car is equipped with automatic transmission, speed control, tilt steering wheel, power disc brakes, AM–FM stereo, rear window defroster, block heater and heavy duty battery. It is assumed that this car is driven 18,000 km per year. The ownership costs of $6,071 per year equate to $16.58 per day.[16]

Average Annual Ownership Costs (Fixed)	
Insurance	$1,191
Licence and registration	$128
Depreciation	$3,974
Finance expense (car loan)	$777
Total	**$6,071**

---

[16] Canadian Automobile Association, 2000 Driving Costs.

Operating costs include items such as gas, oil, and maintenance. These costs are proportional to the amount you drive. For the previously mentioned Cavalier, they are as follows:

Average Operating Costs (Variable)	
Fuel and oil	7¢ per km
Maintenance	3¢ per km
Tires	1¢ per km
Total	**11¢ per km**

The total cost of driving a car is a combination of ownership plus operating costs. The next table shows the annual costs, as per the Canadian Automobile Association, of driving the same Cavalier various distances.

Total Annual Costs			
Km Driven	**Ownership Costs**	**Operating Costs**	**Total Costs**
12,000	$6,071	$1,326	$7,397
18,000	$6,071	$1,989	$8,060
24,000	$6,917	$2,652	$9,569
36,000	$8,044	$3,536	$11,580

The following graph illustrates the same information. It is evident that ownership costs account for the major portion of the expenses. They go up after 18,000 km due to additional depreciation of the vehicle.

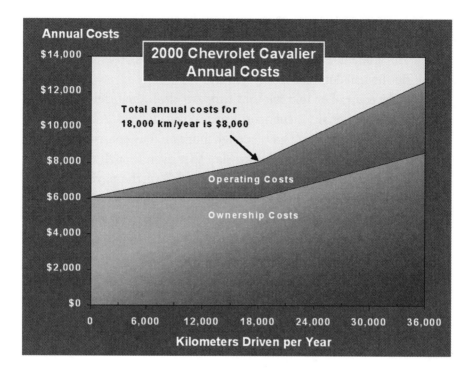

The total cost of owning this car and driving it 18,000 kilometres per year is $8,060. To pay for this expense you must first earn income. But part of your income goes to taxes, leaving you with less to spend.[17] In this case, you would likely have to earn an extra $13,000 to cover the car expense of $8,060.

Ask yourself if it is worth earning $13,000 in extra salary just to support your need to drive this car 18,000 kilometres. Can you buy a used car so your ownership costs are greatly reduced (i.e. cut the size of the bottom box in half)? Can you trade your car in less frequently, again to reduce ownership costs? If you have two vehicles, are you able to make do with just one?

The late Dr. J.C. Taylor, who was my finance professor at the Ivey School of Business in London, really reduced his ownership costs. He got

---

[17] Income taxes are discussed in Chapter 6 and in Chapter 16.

rid of his car altogether. He calculated that he could take a taxi anywhere he wanted to go, including trips to neighbouring cities, and still be money ahead. His students, including myself, thought he was completely out to lunch. But he had done the math, we hadn't.

A credit counsellor told me that cars are often the primary cause of personal financial crisis. A common scenario is as follows. A couple needs a car. They know they don't have enough money to buy one, so they decide to lease. They are under the impression that even though they haven't done the calculations, they must be able to afford the payments if the automobile dealership is willing to set up a lease agreement with them. But often they are in such a financial bind that they can't make the third payment. The company takes back the car, but the couple is still on the hook for all the remaining payments. Bankruptcy is the only way out.

Vehicle costs are being emphasized because many people overspend in this area. But let's look at where we spend the rest of our money. In 1998, the average Canadian household took in and spent a total of $51,361. The following pie chart shows where this money was disbursed.[18]

---

[18] Statistics Canada, Income Statistics Division, "Average Household Expenditures, Canada, Provinces and Territories, 1998". (Statistics Canada Tel: 888–297–7355).

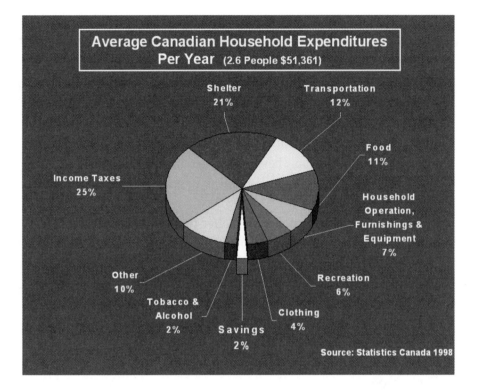

Average Canadian Household Expenditures Per Year (2.6 People $51,361)

Shelter 21%
Transportation 12%
Food 11%
Household Operation, Furnishings & Equipment 7%
Recreation 6%
Clothing 4%
Savings 2%
Tobacco & Alcohol 2%
Other 10%
Income Taxes 25%

Source: Statistics Canada 1998

Compare your household spending to that of the average Canadian household. Where do you already excel at keeping expenditures down? In which areas could you spend less and save more? Note that the pie chart shows that the 2.6 people making up the average Canadian household only managed to save $1,245 per year (2.4% of $51,361).

Remember the goal is to save $6.50 per day. Perhaps it would be easier to think of this as $50 per week, $200 per month, or $2,400 per year. For instance, you may decide to save $50 a week by taking your family out for dinner once instead of twice a week. It is noteworthy that dining at restaurants accounts for 28% of the Canadian food budget[19] and 46% of the U.S. food budget.[20] No matter how you do it, find some way to put aside $2400 a year, and then build it up to $4,000 by buying an RRSP.

---

[19] Statistics Canada, Household Surveys Division, "Average Weekly Food Expenditure per Household, Canada, Regions, Provinces and Selected Metropolitan Areas, 1996".
[20] The Globe and Mail, January 11, 2000.

Remember that by putting $4,000 annually in an RRSP (where it earns 12%) you will amass $76,679 over a ten–year period. (Review the graph in the section "Your Financial Plan" in Chapter 3, "The Basics".)

All our material desires translate into a huge need for a job that will provide us with money. I know a very wealthy person who has his own philosophy on this subject. He believes that many people are "addicted" to their job (dependent on it) because they live from one paycheque to the next. If they lose the job, they are in deep financial trouble. Instead they should develop an independent source of income. He thinks that everyone is capable of doing this.

There are two approaches that offer the best prospects for this independent source of income. The first is to use your savings to buy solid investments. The other way is to start your own business. A primary objective should be to grow the company and hire employees, so that they can generate income for you even if you are absent. Be wary though that if the business is small and depends on your being there, it is really just the same as having a job.

Summary

Limit your material needs and wisely invest the savings. In time, this strategy will free you from all financial worries.

Years Invested	Total Savings
5	$28,461

6

REGISTERED RETIREMENT SAVINGS PLANS

Registered Retirement Savings Plans (RRSPs) were introduced in 1957 to encourage individuals to save for their retirement. An RRSP is a trust that is registered with the government. It can be purchased at any financial institution. The money within an RRSP can be invested in various ways. The big advantage of RRSPs is that they reduce income tax. To understand this, you must first know how tax is calculated. (Taxes will be explained more fully in Chapter 16.)

> "I'm proud to be paying taxes. The only thing is I could be just as proud for half the money."
>
> – Arthur Godfrey

Not all income is taxed equally, and some is not taxed at all. The two most important tax terms that you must become familiar with are "taxable income" and "marginal tax rate". Taxable income, i.e. what you pay taxes on, is your total income less allowed deductions. Marginal tax represents the combined effect of both the federal and provincial income taxes. The following table shows the marginal tax rate payable at various levels of taxable income. Note that the figures have been rounded for simplicity.

Tax Table	
Taxable Income	Marginal Tax Rate
$0 – $7,400	0%
$7,400 – $30,000	25%
$30,000 – $60,000	40%
$60,000 and above	50%

The following graph provides a more visual depiction of this same information.[21]

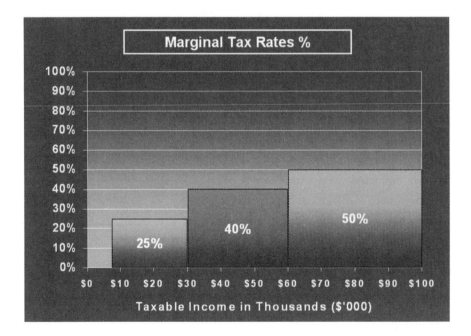

Let's look at this more closely. If you earn less than $7,400, you pay no taxes.[22] If you earn more than $7,400 but less than $30,000, you pay no taxes on the first $7,400, and keep 75 cents of each dollar earned between $7,400 and $30,000 (our governments take the remaining 25

---

[21] The marginal tax rates used are approximations, because they change each year and vary from province to province. The important thing is to understand how marginal tax rates work.
[22] The actual amount for 2001 is $7,416, which was rounded to $7,400 for simplicity.

44

cents). If your annual income is greater than $30,000 and less than $60,000, you pay no taxes on the first $7,400, keep 75 cents of each dollar earned between $7,400 and $30,000, and keep 60 cents of every dollar earned between $30,000 and $60,000. Finally, if you earn more than $60,000 annually, you pay no taxes on the first $7,400, keep 75 cents of each dollar earned between $7,400 and $30,000, keep 60 cents of every dollar earned between $30,000 and $60,000, and keep 50 cents of every dollar earned above $60,000.

Contrary to popular belief, it is always worthwhile to earn more income, as you will never lose more than 50% of it to taxes. Some people think that as they move into a new tax bracket, the higher tax rate will apply to all of their income. As you have seen, this is not true.

RRSPs lower your taxes because they are a deduction from your taxable income. The tax savings are dependent on the amount of RRSPs bought and your marginal tax rate. If your taxable income was $32,000, and it was lowered to $31,000 by purchasing a $1000 RRSP, your marginal tax rate at this level would still be 40% (all income between $30,000 and $60,000). Therefore, you would save 40% of the $1,000 or $400. Your employer had already deducted tax on your $32,000 pay cheque, so the $400 is a refund of tax you have already paid on the $1,000.

Here is a more complicated example. Assume that you still earned $32,000 but instead you bought a $4,000 RRSP. The tax savings are 40% for the first $2,000 but only 25% on the next $2,000. This is because the first $2,000 lowered your taxable income to $30,000, which is still in the 40% marginal tax rate. The second $2,000 reduced your taxable income to $28,000, which puts you in the marginal tax rate of 25% (all income between $7,400 and $30,000). Note that there would be no point in buying RRSPs to decrease your taxable income to less than $7,400. Your marginal tax rate at this point is zero and no tax savings are possible.

When you withdraw money from your RRSP, it is added to your taxable income. For example, if you had $28,000 of taxable income and decided to withdraw $4,000 from your RRSP, your taxable income would now be $32,000. The first $2,000 of the withdrawal would bring your taxable income to $30,000. It would be taxed at 25% (the marginal rate on taxable income less than $30,000). The next $2,000 would bring your taxable income to \$32,000. It would be taxed at the next marginal tax rate, which is 40%.

There is a limit to the amount of RRSPs that you are allowed to buy. This limit is called your "RRSP room". It is calculated yearly, and is the lesser of 18% of your earned income (income from employment, rentals, and self–employment), or \$13,500. If you have a pension plan, the amount your employer has contributed to it is deducted from your available "room". RRSP deductions not used one year may be carried forward and used in subsequent years. There is a seven–year limitation to the carry forward. If you have any doubt as to how much you are allowed to buy, check the assessment that you received from Canada Customs and Revenue Agency, or give them a call. They are very helpful people.

To illustrate the value of saving and using RRSPs, consider the following example. Let's assume that two people, John and Joan, each earn \$40,000 a year. Each manages to save \$6.50 every day (\$2,400 annually). John decides not to use RRSPs, but Joan does. She knows that she will get a tax refund by doing this. So, she takes out a loan in the amount of the tax refund that she expects back i.e. \$1,600. Therefore, she is able to contribute \$4,000 to her RRSP (\$2,400 of savings + \$1,600 from the loan). When she files her tax return, the government will refund her \$1,600 (marginal tax rate of 40% x \$4,000). She uses this refund to pay back the bank for the \$1,600 borrowed. (Less than a month should elapse from the time she borrows the money to the time she obtains her tax refund. The interest cost for the loan should be less than \$15.) Joan, by using an RRSP to her advantage, is able to invest 67% more each year than John (\$4,000 versus \$2,400).

$2,400 Savings $1,600 Tax Refund

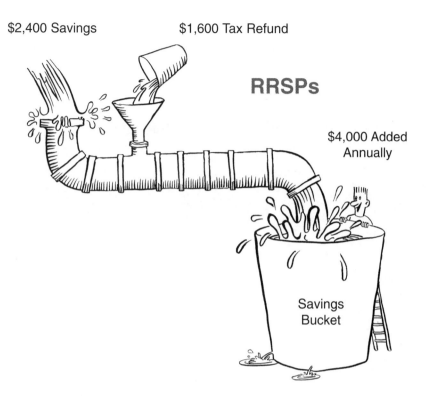

To apply this idea to your own situation, here is a simple way to calculate how much of a loan you need to bump up your RRSP contribution. Multiply the amount of money you have saved to put in an RRSP by .33, .67, or 1.0, depending if your marginal tax bracket is 25%, 40% or 50% respectively. For example, if you have $1,000, and are in the 25% marginal tax rate, you would multiply $1,000 times .33 to get $330. Therefore, you would take out a loan for $330, and contribute a total of $1,330 to an RRSP. You would get back a refund of 25% of $1,330 ($332) to pay back your loan. Because of the refund, you have only spent $1,000 to have $1,330 invested.

Some people buy only enough RRSPs to eliminate any taxes owing on their annual tax return. Others spend their RRSP tax refund as soon as they get it. These folks are missing out on the opportunity to use RRSPs as a focused savings plan.

The following graph is a comparison of Joan and John's results after saving $6.50 a day for 30 years. The rate of return earned throughout the period for both was assumed to be 12%.[23]

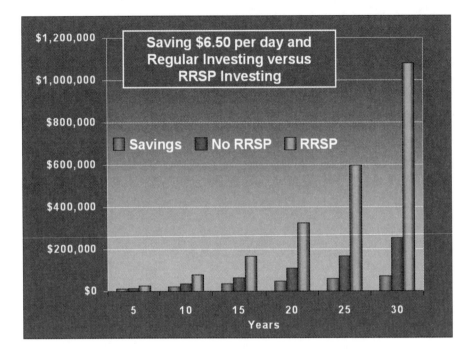

The first thing to notice is the shortest bar at the 30–year point in time. This represents the $72,000 that Joan and John have each saved. The bar next to this one shows that John's savings grew to over $250,000. The last bar – the tallest one in the chart – is Joan's savings, which reached over $1,000,000. The significant eye–opener is that it took only $72,000 of savings for Joan to accumulate over $1,000,000.

There are two reasons why Joan did much better than John. Joan is investing 67% more each year, and none of her earnings inside the RRSP

---

[23] The rate of 12% was chosen because it was felt to be achievable. The last column of the table in Appendix I "Results of Saving $6.50 per Day" shows year–by–year figures for RRSP investment results (for 40 years).

have yet been taxed. They are all added to her investment base and are working for her. On the other hand, John loses 40% of his investment earnings every year to taxes.

For the sake of comparison between Joan and John, let's look at what will happen if Joan now cashes in her entire RRSP at once. (It is extremely unlikely that she would do this. First of all she would not need all the cash at one time. Secondly, doing that would mean that the total amount would be taxed at her highest marginal tax rate of 50%.) If she did cash it in all at once, she would lose $500,000 to taxes. However, this still leaves her with $250,000 more than John, who has already paid the taxes on his savings.

RRSPs offer another advantage to married people. You are allowed to buy an RRSP in either your name, or your spouse's name (spousal RRSP). In either case, you receive the same immediate benefit of a reduction in your taxable income. For example, if you are married and your spouse has a lower taxable income, or does not work outside the home, use a portion of your RRSP room to buy an RRSP in your name, and use the balance to buy a spousal RRSP (your deduction but registered in your spouse's name). The reason for doing this is so that when you and your spouse withdraw money from these RRSPs, you will be minimizing the amount taxed at the top marginal rate. You will each have an equal amount of taxes to pay (at the lower marginal tax rate), as opposed to one spouse paying a lot and the other one paying very little. As much as possible, use spousal RRSPs to equalize retirement income.

Remember that another advantage of RRSPs is that upon the death of one spouse, the RRSP money may be transferred – tax free – to the survivor. Only when the surviving spouse dies must taxes finally be paid.

The money you contribute to an RRSP is usually kept there for a long time. It is therefore important to invest it where you will obtain a high rate of return. Most people know that savings accounts, term deposits and mutual funds are allowed in RRSPs. However, many people are not aware that shares are also permitted.

There is a 30% limit to the amount of foreign content RRSPs can hold. Foreign shares are those of corporations whose head office is not in Canada. For cash investments, non–Canadian dollar deposits are considered foreign. Interestingly, foreign content is based on cost, not market value. If you put $10,000 into your RRSP and $1,000 of that is in foreign shares, they will count as 10% foreign content. If these shares grow to $4,000, you are still on side. If at any time you want to use up the remaining 20% foreign content for that contribution, you may buy another $2,000 of foreign shares. Note that whenever you add more money to your RRSP, 30% of this new amount is added to your existing foreign content room. In the same example, if you add another $10,000 to your RRSP, you will add $3,000 to your unused foreign content room of $2,000 to make a total of $5,000.

Dividends from foreign shares will add to your foreign content, so keep your initial investment slightly below the 30% limit. There is a fine of 1% per month on any amount that is over the limit. Tracking your foreign content may sound complex, but the financial institution that holds your account is required to do this for you.

Foreign content is determined separately for each RRSP account. If you hold two RRSP accounts, and have only taken 10% foreign content on one of them, you cannot make it up by taking over 30% on the other. Therefore, the best way to maximize your foreign content room is to have just one RRSP account.

As a point of interest, it is possible to have 100% foreign content in your RRSP. Most banks offer mutual funds that are invested totally in foreign securities, but are nevertheless classified as Canadian content.

When should you withdraw some money from your RRSP? Not until you require it. Withdraw only the amount that you need to live on, keeping the bulk of it tax sheltered. At age 69, you must close your RRSP. At this point, convert your RRSP into a RRIF (Registered Retirement Income Fund). The foreign content, recalculated on the day the RRIF is created, is limited to 30% of the value held in the RRSP. For example, assume you have $100,000 in your RRSP at the time it becomes a RRIF. If you have foreign shares, e.g. Microsoft, that total more than $30,000, you will have to sell some and buy Canadian shares, such as the Royal Bank, to get back under 30% foreign content. After this date, the foreign content is again based on cost. The $30,000 you have in Microsoft shares could double in value and you would not have to be concerned.

A RRIF is just an RRSP with one more condition attached. This condition requires that you must take out a certain amount each year, like it or not. At age 70, you must withdraw 4.7% of the previous year's ending balance. This rises to 20% of the previous year's balance at age 94, and remains at this rate thereafter. If you wish, you may take out more than the minimum amount prescribed by the RRIF.

It is best not to change the RRSP into a RRIF before it is necessary. There is one exception. Canada Customs and Revenue Agency allows taxpayers who are 65 or older to receive $1,000 of annual pension income tax–free. To obtain this deduction, you must have at least this amount as pension income. (CPP does not count.) If no pension income exists, you can create some by changing some of your RRSP to a RRIF, and then withdrawing $1,000 annually out of the RRIF. How long this tax deduction will be allowed is anyone's guess.

Many Canadian taxpayers don't contribute to RRSPs. Those between 45–54 years of age have the highest rate of participation, but it is only 44%. Just 3% of all contributors use up their allowable limit. They invest their RRSPs as follows: mutual funds 55%, GICs 13%, savings accounts 9%, shares 7%, bonds 5%, other 11%.[24] But this next statistic is the most telling. The amount Canadians invest in RRSPs ($26 billion) is about the same as they spend annually on gambling ($20–$27 billion).[25] Clearly there is room for improvement in the number of people taking advantage of the RRSP tax break, the amount contributed, and how the money is invested.

RRSPs are one of the most effective strategies you can utilize to grow your wealth. If you put your money into an RRSP account instead of a regular bank account, the government (other taxpayers) will give you back about half the money you invested. In effect, an RRSP is a transfer of tax money from taxpayers who do not save to those that do. The only catch is that some day, perhaps 30 years later, you will have to pay taxes on the funds withdrawn. However, you have had the opportunity to save about twice the amount of money (and own the resulting growth), as compared

---

[24] "High–Stake RRSP Race Is On", Financial Post, January 8, 2000.
[25] "Gambling in Canada – A Multi–Billion Dollar Industry", National Council of Welfare, Winter 1996.

to someone who did not take advantage of them. If you have money, and the room to contribute more to an RRSP, take full advantage of it.

Years Invested	Total Savings
6	$36,356

7

INVESTMENT OPTIONS

Now that you have some money set aside, what are your options for investing it? In other words, where should you plant your seedlings so that they will be safe and will grow quickly into big healthy trees? Your main options are: cash investments, fixed income investments, shares, real estate, life insurance, currency positions, and derivatives.

The financial community does not regard gambling as an investment option. But so much money is spent in this area, in an attempt to become wealthy, that it has been included in this chapter.

> "We must learn to explore all the options and possibilities that confront us in a complex and rapidly changing world."
>
> – James William Fulbright

Cash Investments

The essence of a cash investment is that interest is paid to you for the use of your money. At the end of the term, the principal (the money you started with) is returned. However, this investment will not pay any more interest than the amount agreed upon at the outset, no matter how much was made by those who used your money. There is also no chance for a capital gain i.e. your principal does not grow. It is like owning a mature apple tree. Each year you can harvest the apples (interest), but the tree itself (principal) never grows.

One example of a cash investment is a savings account; the interest it earns is quite low. The chartered banks developed a more attractive product called a "term deposit". It earns a higher rate of interest but there are some stipulations. A minimum amount must be invested for a predetermined amount of time; the usual terms are one, two, three, four, or five years. In general, the interest rate increases as the term lengthens. Usually funds can be withdrawn prior to maturity (the end of the term), but there is a penalty.

A similar instrument, called a guaranteed investment certificate or GIC, can be found at trust companies. It too requires a minimum amount invested for a predetermined length of time. Usually it cannot be cashed prior to maturity.

Another common cash investment is the Canada Savings Bond. Each fall since 1946, the government of Canada has sold CSBs through sales agents such as banks and security firms. They are always issued on November 1st. Often there is a limit to the amount an individual may buy, as well as a limit to the total amount the government issues. CSBs must be registered in the name of the person who buys them. This protects the owner against loss, theft or destruction of the certificate. Ownership cannot be transferred. However, at any time CSBs may be cashed for their face value plus accrued interest up to the end of the previous month. Therefore, it is best to cash them just after the start of the month to limit the loss of interest. If you cash them on the 15th of the month, you will lose 15 days interest.

There are two common types of CSBs: regular interest bonds and compound interest bonds. Regular interest bonds come in denominations of $300, $500, $1,000, $5,000 and $10,000 dollars. The interest is physically paid to you each year. Compound interest bonds come in denominations as low as $100. They do not pay the interest to you. Instead, this interest is added to the principal, so you are receiving interest on your interest. Even though you do not physically receive the interest each year from a compound bond, it still must be declared for tax purposes.

The third type of CSB is the RRSP bond, so named because it can only be bought inside an RRSP. It is less flexible, as it can only be cashed on its anniversary date. However, it can be exchanged for a regular CSB. It is issued from early February to April 1st in denominations of $100, $300, $500, $1,000, $5,000, and $10,000.

The Bank of Canada has organized an excellent savings program for CSBs. There are over 18,000 organizations and one million participants who use payroll deduction to buy CSBs. The employee buys the CSB in November and is given a company loan to cover the amount for which he or she cannot pay. The loan plus interest is paid back through payroll deduction. The loan interest is tax deductible, as the employee paid it to earn investment income.

Treasury bills are another popular cash investment. The Minister of Finance auctions them every second week. The amounts range from $1,000 to $1,000,000. They mature in 98, 182 or 364 days. Treasury bills do not pay interest. Instead they are sold at a discount and always mature at their face value. The difference between these two values is what the investor earns; it is treated as interest income for tax purposes. For example, a 98–day treasury bill may sell for $975 and mature at $1,000. The $25 difference is what the investor makes. This low return on investment is the main disadvantage with T–bills.

The liquidity, i.e. how quickly you can convert an investment into money, varies by investment type. For example, a bank account is very liquid, because money can be taken out at any time. By contrast, term deposits lock in your money until the end of the agreed–upon term and are therefore less liquid.

Generally speaking, investors prefer their assets to be liquid. It is possible to obtain the best long–term rate and still remain liquid. For instance, suppose you wanted to invest $10,000 in a term deposit. Rather than investing the full amount for five years, you could invest $2,000 in each of 1, 2, 3, 4 and 5 year terms. As each term ends, you would reinvest the original $2,000 investment, as well as the interest earned, for a new 5–year term. Consequently, within four years, everything will be invested at 5–year rates, and one–fifth of the total investment will come due each year.

The cash deposited in most banks and trust companies is insured by the Canada Deposit Insurance Corporation (CDIC). The amount covered is $60,000 per individual per financial institution. You can confirm that your financial institution carries this insurance by contacting CDIC at 1-800-461-2342. Note that all CSBs and T-bills are automatically guaranteed because the money is being lent to the federal government. A government cannot go bankrupt, as it can always raise more money by increasing taxes.

Fixed Income Investments

Generally, fixed income investments involve much larger sums of money than cash investments. They get their name because their interest rates are fixed for a long period of time. This usually means that they pay higher interest. Another huge difference is that fixed income investments can be readily bought or sold between investors, because ownership can be transferred.

The most common fixed income investment is the bond, not to be confused with a Canada Savings Bond, which is a totally different product. A bond is essentially a standard legal agreement between lender (investor) and borrower (the corporation that needs the money). For example, Air Canada may issue bonds to finance a fleet of new planes. The borrower promises to pay the principal back to the lender at a future date. Interest is paid twice annually. The interest (called the coupon rate) is fixed for the life of the bond and is calculated on the bond's face value, which is always in multiples of $1,000. To ensure the lender's safety, the borrower always pledges assets as security. If a bond goes into default, the lenders will seize the pledged assets and sell them to recover their money. A government does not pledge assets to back up the bond it issues, because its lenders are never worried about not being paid back.

Investors can make or lose a lot of money by speculating in bonds. Speculators are people who buy and sell, with the hope of making a profit from future price changes. Imagine that you bought a $10,000 20–year bond with a 6% coupon rate. If interest rates dropped to 3%, investors would give you much more than $10,000 for your bond that will pay 6% interest for the next 20 years. Similarly, if interest rates shot up to 10%, you are locked in to receiving only 6% for the next 20 years. You could sell your bond, but only at a steep discount from the $10,000 you paid for it. Many investors believe that this volatility makes them more risky than cash investments. This is not the case. If you buy and keep a 6% bond until its maturity, you are certain to receive 6% interest every year plus $10,000 back in 20 years time. Cash investments are as volatile as fixed income investments, but the investor cannot see the gains and losses because there is no marketplace where they are reflected.

The bond market is immense. According to the Canadian Securities Institute, in 1996 the dollar volume traded in the Canadian bond market was 40 times the dollar volume traded in the Canadian stock market.

Debentures are the same as bonds but they do not have specific assets pledged for collateral. Debentures are backed only by the general credit of the borrower. Municipalities often issue debentures.

Shares (Equity)

Much of the world's business is conducted through large corporations e.g. the Royal Bank, Wal–Mart, and General Electric. By selling shares to investors, corporations raise money to help finance business operations. The shareholders collectively share (hence the name) 100% of the ownership of all corporations, be they big or small. Share ownership effectively gives the holder the right to a portion of the corporation's earnings.

It is extremely difficult for anyone to accurately predict a corporation's future earnings. However, assumptions about this are what drive share prices up and down. If investors perceive the corporation will do well, i.e. they expect it to have growing sales and profits, the value of its shares will also grow. Alternatively, if the outlook for the corporation does not look good, there will be little demand for their shares and their value will decline. Investors' perceptions of a corporation's future earnings are subject to sudden changes, often for unknown reasons. The results are dramatic shifts in share value. It is this volatility that frightens many people away from investing in shares. They perceive them as being risky. But are they?

Dr. Jeremy Siegel, Professor at the Wharton School, University of Pennsylvania, would describe them as your safest option. He has done a lot of research to compare the rate of return earned by various investments. He concluded that, "The superiority of shares to fixed income investments over the long run is indisputable." [26]

You can buy shares directly on the stock market. Or you can invest in them indirectly through mutual funds or through exchange–traded funds. These options are discussed in detail later.

Real Estate

Anyone who owns land, a house, a cottage or a building has an investment in real estate. There was a time when real estate investments nationwide did very well. This was when many baby boomers were leaving home and starting their own families. Generally, the "glow" on real estate investment has dimmed in recent years. However, in selected areas it continues to be a lucrative investment.

The main problem with real estate is that it is usually a large investment, and it is not very liquid. Unlike a bank account, where you can write a cheque and take out part of the investment, you have to sell an entire real estate investment to get your hands on any cash. It is also possible that when you need to sell your house or commercial property, you may have difficulty finding a buyer.

Before purchasing real estate, it is important to bear in mind whether the value of the surrounding real estate is appreciating or depreciating, and if this trend is likely to continue. Either way, it will impact on the future value of your property. Also, ask yourself if this property is easily marketable.

Another consideration, and one that people don't often think of, is that real estate is usually held in local dollars. If you need U.S. dollars because you want to spend winters in Florida, and your only income is from Canadian real estate rentals, you may fall short if the Canadian currency falls relative to the U.S. currency. Cash investments and shares allow you to buy assets in a foreign currency. This way, you can have the required savings in U.S. dollars, and you will not have to worry about currency fluctuations.

---

[26] "Stocks for the Long Run", Dr. Jeremy J. Siegel, 1998.

One way around not having your investment in local dollars is to buy U.S. real estate. However, this usually brings with it all sorts of complications, such as absentee management, foreign taxes and foreign laws. These are problems that are best avoided.

Owning rental property is not always an easy way to make money. First of all, as a landlord, you may have a tenant who does not pay the rent. Do you really want the aggravation of evicting someone? Also, having done the tax returns of many landlords, I am always amazed at the amount they spend on repairs and maintenance. The buyer of a rental often underestimates what these costs will be.

It is obvious that I am not too keen on real estate investments. I know very few people who have made money on them. However, I do recommend that you own the roof over your head. If you purchase your own dwelling, then at some point you will no longer be committed to mortgage payments. By that time, you will have accumulated an asset of substantial value. As well, you can live much more inexpensively if you aren't making mortgage or rental payments. So, even if your house or condo does not offer the best return on investment, it is still valuable as a forced savings plan. There is also the bonus of pride in ownership.

Life Insurance

If you require life insurance, by all means purchase a term insurance policy (see Chapter 17, "Insurance"). However, never purchase it solely as an investment for your estate. The insurance companies must make a profit and therefore they keep part of every premium (what you pay each month). If you are looking for an investment that leaves the most to your heirs, there are better options than insurance.

Whole life insurance is different from term insurance in that it takes part of each premium paid and puts it away for you as an investment. One brand name for this insurance is Freedom Fifty–Five. Universal life is the modern version of this concept and is generally more flexible.

The investment part of universal life is usually linked to a term deposit or a stock exchange index (a term that will be explained later). You may stop paying monthly premiums when the invested portion is either earning enough interest to pay for the annual insurance cost, or it equals the death benefit, which is the amount paid to your estate once you pass away. Many policies allow the owner to borrow up to 75% of the invested portion. This may not be as attractive as it appears. If you had invested the money in your own savings account, you could "borrow" 100% of your savings.

The fees charged by universal life policies can be scandalous. The insurance company pays a good portion of these fees to the financial planners who sell their policies. One client of mine invested $18,000 in a universal life policy. She soon lost faith in this investment and requested that her policy be cancelled. In less than a year, fees had reduced her $18,000 investment to $2,000 (a drop of 89%).

At the time my client bought this investment, she was not aware that these fees would be charged. Financial regulators would argue that all fees are fully disclosed in a prospectus that every buyer receives. However, this is a large document and the fee information is buried in the fine print. Few people read it. A sale to my client would never have been made if she had realized the fee structure.

Do yourself a favour; avoid buying whole and universal life insurance policies.

Currency Positions

Most countries have their own currency. Its value fluctuates relative to other currencies. For example, in 1974 the Canadian dollar was worth 4% more than the U.S. dollar; in 2000 it was worth 35% less.

Our true wealth (purchasing power) is dependent upon the assets you have, as well as the value of the currency in which they are held. As a prudent investor, try to diversify your investments so that they are in the currencies you feel will be strongest in the future. If you are unsure, keep the bulk of your investments in one or more of the world's major currencies e.g. the U.S. dollar or the euro.

Here is an example to illustrate what I mean. In 1997, the Indonesian currency (the rupiah) lost 84% of its value relative to the U.S. dollar. Let's compare two Indonesian citizens who each had the equivalent of $100,000 U.S. prior to this. The first kept his assets in local currency i.e. he owned a house. The second citizen rented a house and held her assets in U.S. dollars, e.g. Intel shares or U.S. dollar bonds. After the currency devaluation, she still had $100,000. The first person was left with assets valued at only $16,000 (16% of $100,000).

Currency fluctuations offer the opportunity for investors to make or lose a lot of money. If they think a currency is under valued, they buy more of it now and sell it once it has appreciated. If they think it is over valued, they sell it now and buy it back after it has depreciated. However, the average investor should not speculate on currency changes. It is much too risky.

Derivatives

A derivative is any financial product that derives its value from another product. It is bought and sold on stock and commodity exchanges much like a share. But while a share has value because it owns something (part of a corporation), a derivative derives its value solely because it has *the right* to own something e.g. a share.

A call option is one popular derivative. It is set up between two investors by a brokerage firm. This derivative gives the buyer the right to buy 100 shares (or multiples thereof) within a specified time. The seller collects a fee for this. Once the call option is issued, it trades on the stock exchange until it expires. Its price is very volatile.

Suppose Microsoft shares are trading at $70. The owner of some of these shares sells a call option for a fee of $5 per share. This permits the buyer to purchase Microsoft shares from the owner for $90 per share within the next three months. The buyer is willing to purchase the derivative, because he expects the value of the shares to rise above $95 during the next three months. The owner wants to sell an option because he does not expect the share price to go as high as $90. He makes $5 per share and has the opportunity to repeat the process every three months.

Assume that after just two months, the Microsoft shares have gone up to $150. The original $5 call option would now trade for $60 ($150 – $90). The buyer may choose to sell this option on the market, or he can exercise his option to buy the shares for $90 each. The seller keeps his $5 per share fee. However, he must sell his Microsoft shares for $90 when they are trading for $150.

If the Microsoft shares are trading for less than $90 at the expiry date, the option simply expires. The buyer loses the $5 per share fee that he paid for the option. The seller is the winner because he pockets the fee and the option expires.

A put option is the opposite of a call option, in that it provides its owner with the right to sell instead of buy shares. To continue with the original example of a $70 Microsoft share, the put option permits the buyer to sell Microsoft shares for $50 per share within the next three months. The buyer expects the shares to decrease in value. The seller is not as pessimistic.

Buyers and sellers can make a lot of money in a short time by using options, but it is very risky.

Futures are another type of derivative. This legally binding contract is a commitment to deliver or take delivery of a stated amount of a specified commodity at some agreed upon date in the future. (Commodities are basic items or staple goods that are bought and sold. Examples include grain, oil, gold, silver, cattle and soybeans.)

The commodity markets function like a stock exchange. The two largest commodity exchanges in North America are both located in Chicago. They are the Chicago Board of Trade and the Chicago Mercantile Exchange. The Winnipeg Commodity Exchange is the only one in Canada.

People trade the rights (ownership) to commodities to make money; many fortunes have been made and lost in this market. One famous example was the rush on tulip bulbs in Holland in the 1630's. The flower–loving Dutch imported these bulbs from Constantinople. Demand outstripped supply, and many people began buying them purely as an investment. The price of tulip bulbs kept going up. A single bulb could fetch the price of 12 sheep or 1,000 pounds of cheese. Suddenly in 1637, the Dutch realized the absurdity of these prices. The value of the bulbs plunged overnight, wiping out the wealth of many individuals. In fact, so many people were involved in this market disaster that it temporarily crushed Holland's economy.

Another more recent example was the attempt by the Hunt family of Texas to corner the silver market in 1979. They tried to buy up the world's supply of silver at low prices. Their plan was to let only limited quantities onto the market at very high prices, and thereby make a fortune. But they ran short of money before the plan could be completed, and lost a bundle instead.

Farmers, like my relatives in Manitoba, do use commodity markets to lock in the price they will receive for their produce, be it grain, honey or something else. The price of these products changes from day to day on the commodity market. As a farmer plants his crops in springtime, he may be happy with the price of wheat. To protect himself from a possible decrease in price, he decides to sell his expected wheat production in the spring for delivery in the fall. This is known as a future, or a fall delivery contract. A company such as Robin Hood Flour would be interested in buying this contract to lock in their cost of raw materials.

Let's assume that in the spring the farmer sells a contract for fall delivery of 100,000 bushels of wheat at $1 per bushel. Should he produce 120,000 bushels, he will fulfill his contract and have a surplus of 20,000 bushels to sell at the market price.

If he has only managed to produce 80,000 bushels by fall, he must then buy 20,000 bushels at the going rate to fulfill his contract. If he has to buy this wheat at $1.10 a bushel, he will lose ten cents a bushel or $2,000. Besides, he receives only a dollar a bushel by having the contract; he would have received the going rate of $1.10 if he had not bought the contract. So he lost ten cents a bushel or $8,000 on the 80,000 bushels he produced.

If the fall price has dropped to 90 cents a bushel and he has only produced 80,000 bushels, he would still be $8,000 ahead. This is because he gets a $1.00 per bushel instead of 90 cents. But he has a contract for 100,000 bushels. So he will also make an additional $2,000 because he can buy 20,000 bushels at 90 cents per bushel and sell it at $1 per bushel.

Any investor can use futures to try to make some money. He can sell a fall contract months in advance for $1 a bushel. When the fall arrives, because he is an investor and not a farmer, he must buy the wheat to fulfill his contract obligation. He will make money if his contract delivery price is higher than the going market rate, and he will lose money if the opposite is true. This process is known as speculating, or gambling on whether the price of wheat will go up or down. The farmer, on the other hand, was not speculating. He was locking in a price that he found acceptable.

The commodity's ownership does not change until the closing date, at which time the goods must be delivered. But in reality, physical deliveries are rare; 98% of all contracts are settled only with money.

The commodity market is a very specialized field, and definitely not an area in which the average person should invest. It takes insight, discipline, nerves of steel, and lots of cash to make money from commodities. However, certain people, providing they have in depth knowledge of a specific commodity, can do well. One individual I knew ran a manufacturing company that used a great quantity of copper. After many years, he became expert at monitoring the key variables that affected this commodity's future price. He would advise his company to buy the rights to copper when its price was low. Therefore, their product costs were less than that of their competitors, and the company was very successful.

To sum up, derivatives are fascinating but complicated investments. Fortunes can be made or lost quickly by using these products. No one but the most experienced investors should invest in them.

Gambling

It may seem strange to include gambling as an investment option, but Canadians spend a lot of money in this area with the hope of striking it rich. The National Council on Welfare estimates annual gambling expenditures to be $20 – $27 billion.[27] Spending in this area is growing rapidly. According to Statistics Canada, the amount spent on gambling doubled between 1992 and 1997. Eighty–two percent of households engage in this activity. In 1997, Statistics Canada calculated that the provincial governments had a net income of $3.8 billion from gambling revenue.[28]

The amount of money spent on gambling demonstrates that there is no shortage of money, just a shortage of knowledge. If this problem can be rectified, the financial well being of millions of Canadians will be greatly improved.

---

[27] "Gambling in Canada – A Multi–Billion Dollar Industry", National Council of Welfare, Winter 1996.
[28] "The Gambling Industry: Raising The Stakes", Statistics Canada, K. Marshall, August 1999.

A lottery corporation keeps 50% of total ticket sales for administration costs, taxes, profits and payouts to charities. The other 50% is paid out to the winners. This is the way all gambling works.

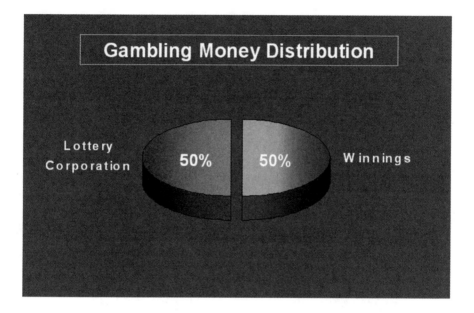

In other words, for every dollar paid in, only 50 cents is available for payout. If the lottery corporation immediately refunded you 50 cents when you bought your $1 ticket, your poor return on investment would be evident. It is much more difficult to see how bad an investment gambling is when the total prize money is "refunded" to only a few of the purchasers. The lure of this big prize clouds people's thinking, and they overestimate their chances of winning. This is an example of "probability blindness". This concept (where people cannot correctly assess the odds) is discussed in detail in Chapter 14, "Risk".

Here's another way of looking at gambling. Assume the lottery corporation estimates that it will sell 2 million tickets at one dollar each. The prize would then be $1 million (50% of $2 million). To guarantee that you win the $1 million prize, would you buy all the tickets for $2 million? Obviously not. Your prize would only be worth half of what you pay in. In lotteries, as in all gambling, the players as a group lose because they always put in more than they take out. The following diagram illustrates how the game works.

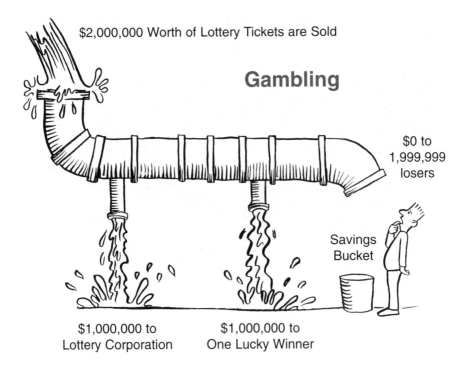

$2,000,000 Worth of Lottery Tickets are Sold

Gambling

$0 to 1,999,999 losers

Savings Bucket

$1,000,000 to Lottery Corporation

$1,000,000 to One Lucky Winner

Going to bingo or betting on horse races can be a form of recreation. My mother loves playing bingo (and guts poker, which she claims she is good at) with her friends every Sunday night. However, she sets a spending limit for herself before she goes. If you are going to gamble for entertainment, consider doing the same.

To reach a destination, it is important to continually move towards it. Every dollar spent gambling is similar to taking a step away from where you want to go. So instead of taking money out of your wallet to buy a lottery ticket, put it in your pocket. Use this money to buy an RRSP. Remember that by saving $6.50 a day, and earning 12% annually, you will have over $1 million in 30 years. (For details, see the last column of the table in Appendix I.) For comparison, assuming you made the same investment in a lottery that pays out half of its revenues in winnings, you would have to play an average of 843 years before you accumulated $1 million.

Years Invested	Total Savings
7	$45,199

8

WHAT TO DO

Now that all the investment options have been covered, let's eliminate those that are not suitable. Gambling is clearly not a good place to "invest" money. Life insurance should not be used as an investment tool. Real estate investments are not liquid and usually do not provide great returns. Derivatives and currency positions are much too speculative to be considered. The only viable alternatives are cash investments, fixed income investments and shares. How do you choose between these three?

"Choice, not chance, determines one's destiny."

– Unknown

The real choice boils down to this simple question. Do you want to be a "loaner" or an "owner"? When you choose cash or fixed income investments, you are lending your money. The borrower, often a bank, provides you with a predictable rate of return for the use of your cash.

When you buy shares, you actually own part of a corporation. You take on all the risks of ownership, but you reap the rewards as well.

One way to decide which of the three investments to choose is to compare their past performance. The following four graphs demonstrate the rate of return for cash investments, fixed income investments and shares during the last 200, 50, 10 and 5 years.

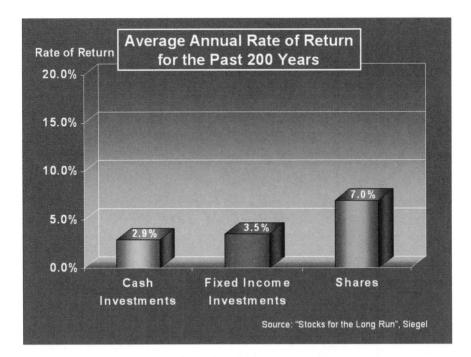

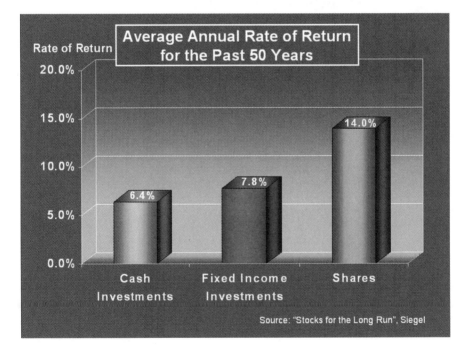

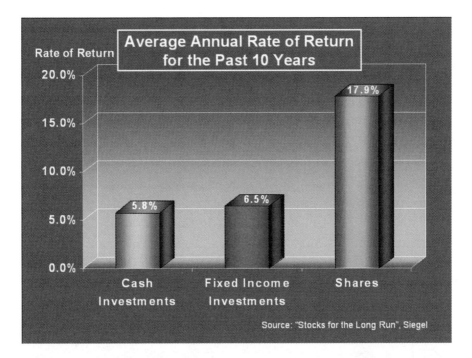

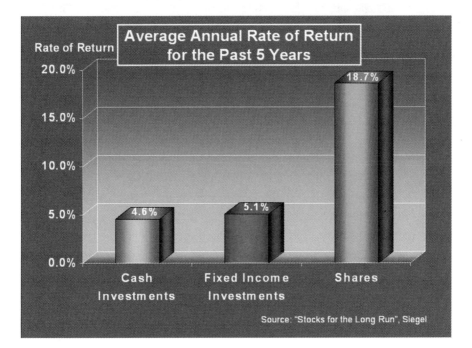

Regardless of the time frame, it is clear that shares were tops and cash investments had the poorest results. It is important to note that the graphs do not address the impact of taxes. Income from shares is taxed at a much lower rate than income from cash investments. (This subject will be discussed in detail in Chapter 16, "Income Taxes".) This tax advantage, coupled with their superior rate of return, makes shares the obvious investment choice.

The following table is based on the work done by Dr. Siegel.[29] He calculated the 1997 value of a $1 invested in 1802 in each of cash, fixed income and shares. He demonstrated that a slight difference in the rate of return makes a tremendous difference to the end value. (The rates of return and resulting values were adjusted to exclude inflation. This is the fairest and most meaningful method of comparing numbers over a long period of time.)

Investment Comparisons 1802–1997		
$1 Invested in 1802	Rate of Return	Value in 1997
Cash Investments	2.9%	$275
Fixed Income Investments	3.5%	$803
Shares	7.0%	$559,000

Shares are the clear winner in terms of rate of return. Dr. Siegel recommends that even conservative investors should have nearly 90% of their investments in shares. But how comfortable are you with volatility? Will you become fearful and have trouble sleeping at night if the value of your investments fluctuates a lot? If so, you may have to stay with cash investments. However, if you can overcome your fear and be content with shares, you will drastically increase your long–term investment growth.

---

[29] "Stocks for the Long Run", Dr. Jeremy Siegel, 1998.

In the future, investments in shares may do even better than they have in the past. This is due to the influence of "baby boomers", a huge group of people born in Australia, Canada and the United States between 1947 and 1966. Baby boomers have had a major impact on the economy. For example, when they wanted to buy homes, the increased demand drove house prices and interest rates sky high. Now in 2001, the lead baby boomers are 54 years old. Their expenses are down because, for the most part, their houses are paid for and their children have left home. These baby boomers are also in their prime earning years, so this, coupled with decreased expenses, means that they have a lot of disposable income. In addition, they are starting to inherit their parents' wealth. (Their parents are the first in history to have significant assets to bequeath.) Consequently, the amount of money available for investing is sharply increasing, and will continue to do so over the next 20 years, as more and more baby boomers approach middle age. Where will they choose to invest all their money? Cash and fixed income investments will not be attractive, because interest rates will likely remain low. The most appealing invest-ment option will be shares. This unprecedented surge of money into the stock market bodes well for future share prices.

There are other advantages to investing in shares. First, they are one of the most liquid investments that you can make. If you want cash, sim-ply direct your broker to sell some of your shares, and you will have your money within three days. Second, shares are easy to handle. You do not have to watch for maturity dates and re–invest them as you do with fixed income investments. Finally, shares offer the luxury of flexibility. You can sell any portion of your investment, or all of it, at any time you choose.

Shares will be discussed in more detail in Chapter 10.

Years Invested	Total Savings
8	$55,103

9

THE FINANCIAL MARKETPLACE

The financial marketplace is where you buy shares, bonds or other investments. It originated as a meeting place for people who were willing to temporarily lend money, for a fee, to those that wished to borrow it. To facilitate this transfer between people who did not know each other, financial instruments such as shares, bonds, and term deposits evolved. These instruments, often called securities, are really just formal legal documents that set out the rights and obligations of both parties. They have common features that allow everyone to quickly understand them. Financial products are constantly evolving to keep up with our needs.

"The essence of America is the hope to first make money...then make money with money...then make lots of money with lots of money."
– Paul Erdman

The financial market is divided into four main product types: money markets (short term cash investments), bond markets (longer term cash investments), stock markets (shares of companies) and commodity markets (products used in commerce).

There are two other ways to categorize the financial marketplace. First, are prices determined by an open auction or by investment dealers?

Second, who is selling the product i.e. is it a primary or secondary market? Let's look at these definitions.

Auction versus Dealer Markets
Auction Markets

All large stock exchanges operate similarly to other auctions and hence are called auction markets. At these central locations, people make competitive bids and offers (also called asks) in order to exchange money for shares. Stock exchanges are often owned and operated by member investment dealers (commonly referred to as brokerage firms).

Currently, there are about 200 stock exchanges in over 60 nations in the world e.g. London, Hong Kong, and Nikkei (in Tokyo). The New York Stock Exchange (NYSE) and American Stock Exchange (Amex) are both based in New York City. The Nasdaq (National Association of Security Dealers Automated Quotation) is headquartered in Gaithersburg, Maryland. In Canada, there is the Toronto Stock Exchange (TSE), the Montreal Exchange, and the CDNX (Canadian Venture Stock Exchange), which is in Vancouver. There are 4,000 corporations listed on all the stock exchanges in Canada, compared to 29,000 listed on exchanges worldwide. If you choose not to buy shares on foreign stock exchanges, you are ruling out the vast majority of available investment opportunities.

The TSE is Canada's largest exchange, accounting for 85% of all shares traded, measured by dollar value. This may sound impressive, but by world standards the TSE is not big. There are only 1,400 corporations listed, and its dollar volume is just 3% of the Nasdaq.[30] Bigger stock exchanges are better, because they tend to enforce stricter regulations. These rules help to protect the average investor.

A corporation may list its shares on more than one stock exchange. It does this to get more exposure, in hope that its share price will go up. For example, the Royal Bank is listed on the TSE and NYSE. The Nasdaq exchange includes about 160 corporations that are also listed on the TSE. The difference in share prices between two exchanges provides the oppor-

---

[30] During 2000, the TSE had a trading volume of $943 billion Canadian. The Nasdaq had a trading volume of $20.4 trillion U.S.

tunity for arbitrage. This is the practice of buying shares on the stock exchange where they are trading at a lower value, and selling them on the one where they are trading at a higher price. Arbitrage helps to maintain similar share prices on all exchanges.

Dealer Markets

Prices for products on this market are determined by an agreement between investment dealers. There is no central location to a dealer market. Two large dealer markets are the bond and money markets.

Unlisted exchanges (over–the–counter) are also dealer markets. In Canada, the over–the–counter exchange is known as the Canadian Dealing Network Inc. It is small and there is little regulation.

If you have ever received an unsolicited phone call suggesting you buy a hot stock, the share was probably on an unlisted exchange.

Primary versus Secondary Markets

Primary market

The primary market describes a transaction whereby a corporation sells its shares to the general public in order to raise money. For example, when Sam Walton wanted to expand Wal–Mart faster than internally generated money would allow him to do so, he sold part of his ownership.

An "initial public offering" (IPO) is when a corporation offers shares to the public for the first time. Subsequent sales of more shares by the corporation to investors are called "public offerings". The issuing corporation works with a brokerage firm to determine the price and issue date for the new shares. These are complex decisions with enormous financial consequences. Naturally, management wants to sell the shares for the highest possible price, but at the same time it is important that the new issue be completely sold so that they get the money they need. If the corporation sells the new shares at $10 each, and the share price immediately goes up to $20, it is obvious that the shares were under priced when issued. The corporation could have earned double the money had they read the market correctly and issued the shares at $20 instead of $10.

A brokerage firm either charges a fee for its service or, more frequently, it acts as a principal by underwriting the new shares. This means it buys the new shares at a discount from the company and resells them to the general public for a profit. Note that there is a possible conflict of interest. An investment advisor (employee of the brokerage firm) may suggest you buy shares that are owned by the firm she is working for.

Be careful before buying a primary issue. It is not uncommon for them to decrease in value during their first year, once the hype settles down.

Secondary Market

This is the market that we all know and is most often discussed on talk shows and in financial newspapers. Trading of previously issued securities takes place between two investors. The investor selling the shares, not the corporation whose shares are being sold, receives the money from the investor buying the shares. The involvement of a corporation in the secondary market is minimal. It simply records a different owner's name for the share that was traded.

The person selling the share is betting that its price will go down in value, while the person buying the share is betting it will go up. Both people believe that they are doing the right thing or the trade would never take place. No matter what happens, the brokerage firms and their agents (investment advisors), always stand to gain. They receive a commission from both the buyer and the seller every time a trade is made. They want to see lots of trading, as it is the dollar value traded, not the direction of the market, that has a direct impact on their earnings.

There are three distinct ways brokerage firms handle trades. They have the option of acting as an agent for either the buyer or the seller, as an agent for both the buyer and the seller (cross), or as a principal.

Agent: In the secondary market, the brokerage firms usually act as agents i.e. they are merely an intermediary between two investors – the buyer and the seller. The process of transferring ownership of shares begins when a buyer and a seller each place an order with their respective investment advisors. These orders are forwarded to the appropriate stock exchange. As soon as a computer matches price and quantity between buyer and seller, the shares are exchanged. Settlement and confirmation of the transaction follow within three business days. Settlement means the shares have been paid for and ownership has been transferred. (By using the Internet, investors can now place these orders directly themselves without speaking to an investment advisor. However, the transaction must still be put through a brokerage firm.)

Cross: A second type of trade, called a "cross", occurs when one brokerage firm matches a buy order and a sell order between two of its own clients. These transactions do not occur at the stock exchange, but the figures are tabulated and included in the exchange's statistics for the following day. Large investors such as pension funds often trade this way. Again, the role of the brokerage firm is that of an agent. In return for the service of bringing the buyer and seller together, a commission is charged to both parties.

Principal: A brokerage firm is acting as a principal when it buys shares in the market to sell later for a profit. There is an obvious conflict of interest because the firm is competing to get the best buy or sell price for itself, while at the same time acting as an agent for its clients. Investors may not be aware when their brokerage firm is acting as a principal.

Investor Protection

Shares are bought and sold by the brokerage firm in street name. This means that your shares are registered in its name, not yours. To protect their customers, the brokerage firms are required to keep your shares separate from their own. Therefore, even if the firm starts to have financial difficulty, the theory is that they cannot grab your shares to pay their bills.

Brokerage firms contribute to and operate the Canadian Investor Protection Fund. It protects investors for up to $1 million per investor account in case a member brokerage firm runs off with its clients' money. Ontario has had three large payouts. The largest was in 1987, when $15 million was paid out because of the failure of Osler Inc.

The Investment Dealers Association (IDA) is a self–regulatory organization that governs the conduct of its approximately 200 members (brokerage firms). Remember these firms also run the stock exchanges. The IDA states that its purpose is the protection of investors, but undoubtedly its top priority is to protect its members.

In the United States, the Securities and Exchange Commission (SEC) is a federal body established by the U.S. Congress. It sets the rules and regulations governing the financial markets in order to protect its citizens. We have no such federal body in Canada. The only legislation that does exist is provincial. The largest and most aggressive body appears to be the Ontario Securities Commission. But to a large extent it allows the security industry to police itself. In short, Canada has no national arms–length organization whose primary mandate is to look after the interests of investors.

Years Invested	Total Savings
9	$66,195

10

SHARES

Nothing will help you to understand shares better than learning to decipher the stock market quotations. Information about the previous day's events is published daily in financial newspapers. Let's assume you want to find out more about BCE Inc. (Bell Canada Enterprises). It is traded on the Toronto Stock Exchange. Look for the TSE stock quotations in the financial section of a paper such as The Globe and Mail or National Post, and then find the name of the corporation within that exchange's alphabetical listing.

> **"You pays your money and you takes your choice."**
> **– Punch**

The same information is presented for free on the Internet by most banks, stock exchanges, Microsoft, Yahoo, and many other corporations. These sites contain the current market prices and other relevant data, including the latest corporate news and industry analyses. Some Internet addresses are The Toronto Stock Exchange http://tse.com/, The New York Stock Exchange http://nyse.com/, The Nasdaq http://www.nasdaq.com/, and the American Stock Exchange http://amex.com/. At these sites, you can establish your own portfolio for tracking.

Following is a share listing with an explanation of what each column means.

365-day high low		Stock	Sym	Div	High	Low	Close	Chg	Vol (100s)	Yield	P/E Ratio
44.90	30.95	BCE	BCE	1.20	44.90	43.60	44.05	0.05	39,137	2.7%	5:1

high low: BCE Inc. has traded as high as $44.90 and as low as $30.95 in the past 365 days.

Stock: the abbreviated name of the corporation.

Sym: the symbol that the Toronto Stock Exchange uses.

Div: the dividend that the corporation has paid out during the past year.

High Low: during the day under review, the stock traded as high as $44.90 and as low as $43.60.

Close: the last trade of the day was at $44.05.

Chg: short for change. The last trade for the day was 5 cents higher than the one of the previous day.

Vol: volume expressed in hundreds; 3,913,700 shares were traded that day.

Yield: is the annual dividend divided by the close price of the share, expressed as a percentage ($1.20 divided by $44.05 = 2.7%). This calculation gives the effective rate of return that your dividends are providing.

P/E Ratio (Price/Earnings): is the close price per share divided by the earnings per share (not shown in the table). Earnings per share (EPS) is just what it says i.e. earnings reported by the corporation during the past year, divided by the number of shares outstanding. The 5 to 1 P/E ratio in this example is low by industry standards. For example, Coke has traded at 80 times earnings.

The financial paper also provides a separate listing per stock exchange for all shares that had no trades for that day. These corporations are presented in alphabetical order with the bid and ask prices. Also frequently printed is a listing of any shares that hit a new 52–week high or low.

Voting Privileges

One of the most sacred privileges of owning shares is the right to vote. As a part owner of the corporation, you annually elect the directors. On your behalf, the directors oversee the operations of the corporation and its management. Shareholders also have the right to vote on important matters such as the purchase or sale of another business by the corporation.

If a corporation has more than one class of shares, very likely one of them has restricted voting rights. Some examples are:

Non–voting: owners of these shares cannot vote.

Subordinate voting: these shares provide limited voting rights e.g. one–tenth of a vote.

Restricted voting: there is a cap on the number of shares one person can control e.g. a foreigner cannot own more than 20% of a Canadian bank.

Be aware that the Board of Directors issues shares with restricted voting rights in order to minimize the influence shareholders have. As an investor, you want the least restrictions; that way you will have a voice, should you wish to be heard.

Dividends

Dividends are not a contractual obligation. They are paid out only if the Board of Directors decides to do so. In theory, if a corporation has money in excess of its needs, it pays this amount as dividends to its shareholders. But in practice, the corporation's cash position has nothing to do with it. The corporations pay out a dividend regardless of their liquidity at the time. The amount of the dividend tends to remain fixed, because investors favour shares that have a long history of steady dividends. A corporation tends to lower its dividends only if it is in financial trouble.

If the shares are registered in the name of the owner, the dividend money is sent directly to the investor via cheque or direct deposit. But most shares are held in street name. In that case, the corporation sends a large cheque to the brokerage firm, where the money is divided and then deposited to the investors' accounts.

A corporation announces it will pay a dividend to all shareholders at a precise time and date, say 4:00 p.m., July 15th. This date is called the "dividend record date". All investors who own shares at that time receive the dividend. But ownership of shares is constantly changing, and this makes sending the dividends to the correct investor a bit of a challenge. Keep in mind that it takes three days for a transaction between buyer and seller to clear. If you buy a share three days or more prior to the dividend record date, you will be the recipient of the dividend. These shares are said to trade "cum dividend" which means with the dividend. But if you buy a share two days or less before the dividend record date, the dividend will be sent to the previous shareowner, not you. The share is said to trade "ex dividend" or without dividend.

Shareholders tend to have too much faith in dividends, believing that they are getting a bonus, but this is really not the case. Assume 100 shareholders each have one share of a corporation whose only asset is $1,000 in the bank. The fair value of the share is $10 ($1,000 divided by the 100 shares). We will assume that the share trades on the stock exchange at the same value, which is often the case. If a $1 dividend is paid to each of the 100 shareholders, only $900 is left in the corporate bank account. The value of each share is now $9 ($900 divided by 100 shares). This same scenario is evidenced in the real world on the stock market. Shares fall in value by the amount of the dividend as soon as they are trading ex dividend. Shareholders are really no better off after receiving the dividend than they were before.

Some corporations have an optional "dividend reinvestment plan". It allows the shareholders to use their dividends to buy more shares, instead of receiving cash. Sometimes a corporation issues a "stock dividend". In effect this forces all shareholders to participate in the dividend reinvestment plan. In either case, there is no advantage to the investor. The participants have more shares, but the value per share goes down by an equal amount.

Stock splits are similar to stock dividends. A stock split occurs when the shareholders approve a by-law that grants multiple shares e.g. 2, 3, 5,

10 etc. for every one share that the shareholder already has. For example, suppose a corporation has a share worth $10 and elects to have a 2 for 1 stock split. Each share would become 2 shares worth $5 each. Stock splits remind me of what Yogi Berra said when asked if he wanted his pizza cut into 4 or 8 slices. Tongue in cheek he replied, " I am hungry today so cut my pizza into 8 slices." Berkshire Hathaway, the company run by the legendary investor Warren Buffett, has never had a stock split. Its shares, among the most successful ever, trade at $70,000 U.S. ($105,000 Canadian).

The opposite of a stock split is called a reverse split or consolidation. It is when the shareholders decide to consolidate 2, 3, 5 etc shares into one. Corporations do reverse splits with penny stocks i.e. shares that have a low market value. By doing this, it is hoped that their shares will gain respect in the financial marketplace and rise in price. Reverse splits are as meaningless as stock splits.

Share Buy Backs

Sometimes corporations buy back their own shares. These "share buy backs" decrease the number of common shares, thus increasing the percentage of earnings given to the remaining shareholders. Share buy backs are used to supply shares for dividend reinvestment and employee share option plans. But management can also use them to artificially drive up share price. Some people like Warren Buffet strongly oppose this.

Liquidity

Shares of large corporations are extremely liquid i.e. easily sold. For example, Microsoft and Intel often have more than 30 million shares traded daily. The ability to sell shares for cash at short notice makes them an appealing investment.

You can ascertain how liquid a share is by examining its volume i.e. the number of shares traded daily. The shares of some corporations are "thinly traded", meaning their volume is low. Often these corporations are small or unexciting, and therefore not many investors think about investing in them. Or it could be that the people who started the corporation control a large block of shares, leaving only a small portion available to trade. Thinly traded shares are difficult to buy or sell.

Shares of private corporations (those that are not listed on a stock exchange) are extremely non–liquid because there is no public place where such shares are traded. It is not wise to invest in situations like this where there is no easy exit.

How to Buy Shares

All shares must be traded through a brokerage firm that is a member of the stock exchange. You can go to full–service brokers such as (largest first) Nesbitt Burns Group, CIBC World Markets, RBC Dominion Securities Group, TD Securities, ScotiaMcLeod Inc., Merrill Lynch Canada Inc., Lévesque Beaubien Geoffrion, Fahnestock Viner Holdings Inc., First Marathon Inc., Yorkton Securities Inc. and Versus Technologies Inc. (For an up to date listing of firms registered to sell securities, visit the web site of the Ontario Securities Commission www.osc.gov.on.ca.) These brokers will discuss your investment needs and help you decide which shares to buy. You then deposit money in an account, similar to a bank account, opened at the brokerage firm. An investment order will be issued to purchase shares on your behalf. The money for the cost of the shares, and the commission for the broker, will be withdrawn from your account. A few days later, you will receive written confirmation of your purchase.

Another option is to go to a discount broker. They charge less than the full–service firms, but they provide no investment advice. You can open an account with them by filling out a form. All buy and sell orders are handled via their 1–800–telephone number, or through the Internet. The most expensive method is to talk to a telephone representative in person. This will usually cost about $35 plus a percentage of the amount of money you are investing. It is less expensive to use their automated voice system to place an order. You do everything yourself using prompts on the telephone. The easiest and least expensive way to buy or sell shares is to use the Internet. The procedures for settlement of the buy or sell order are the same as with a full service broker. Following is a list of discount brokers and their website addresses:

- Bank of Montreal InvestorLine® http://www.investorline.com
- Charles Schwab Canada   http://www.schwabcanada.com
- CIBC Investor's Edge   http://www.investorsedge.cibc.com
- Disnat (a division of Desjardins Securities) http://www.disnat.com
- E*TRADE Canada   http://www.canada.etrade.com
- HSBC InvestDirect   http://www.hsbcinvestdirect.com
- National Bank Invesnet   http://www.invesnet.com
- Royal Bank Action Direct   http://www.actiondirect.com
- Scotia Discount Brokerage Inc. http://www.sdbi.com
- Sun Life Securities   http://www.sunsecurities.com
- TD Waterhouse   http://www.tdwaterhouse.ca/index.html
- eNorthern   http://www.enorthern.com

There are two types of accounts that either a discount or full service broker will open for you. In a "cash account" the investor pays cash for the shares as soon as they are bought. A "margin account" allows the investor to buy shares on credit by borrowing from the brokerage firm.

As more and more investors are placing orders themselves through discount brokers or via the Internet, it is important to understand the terminology:

At the Market Order: an order to buy or sell at the best market price. This involves paying the ask price if you are buying and accepting the bid price if you are selling.

Limit Order: an order on which a limit is set on what will be paid for shares or a minimum that must be obtained before selling these shares.

Day Order: an order that is only valid for the day it is made. All orders are considered day orders unless otherwise specified.

Open or Good Till Cancelled: this order remains in effect until cancelled. To limit the number of such orders in the system, they are usually set to automatically cancel after 30, 60 or 90 days.

All or None Order: has a restriction placed on it before it can be executed e.g., there may be a restriction on the number of shares that must be bought or sold.

Any Part Order: any part of this order will be accepted in an effort to fill the order.

Good Through Order: an order that is good for a specified number of days, then automatically cancelled.

Stop Loss Order: an order to sell, which comes into effect if the share price drops to a certain level. These orders may not provide as much protection as an investor believes. For example, if the share price drops rapidly, there may be no one willing to buy shares at the price you specify, so the sell order will be filled at a much lower price. Also, your shares can drop in value, be sold and then immediately go back up in value.

Stop Buy Order: the opposite of a stop loss order. This is done to protect a short position (explained in next paragraph) in case the share price starts to rise. The same risks that face a stop loss order also face a stop buy order.

Short Selling

Owning shares is referred to as a "long position". A "short position" is when you sell shares that you do not own. In a long position, you make money if the shares go up in value. In a short position, you make money if the shares go down.

Let's assume that you contact a brokerage firm and place an order to sell short. They will lend you shares for you to sell. The proceeds from this sale, plus an additional 50% of this sale amount, must be deposited by you into your margin account and left there until your short position is cancelled. You are also responsible for paying any dividends declared while you hold the short position. To pay back the person you borrowed from, you must buy shares. You hope that you can buy them for less than you have sold them for, thereby making a profit. The more the share has gone down in value, the less it will cost you to buy the shares to discharge your obligation. The extra 50% you deposited is to protect the brokerage firm in the event that the shares go up in value. If they do, you are required to add more money to your account so that the purchase is covered.

An investor may decide to have a long position in one share and a short position in another. It is possible for an investor to hold on to a short position for a long time. But few do, as this is seen as being risky. In a long position, the most you can lose is what you paid for the share. In a short position, there is no limit on how much you can lose, as there is no limit on how high a share price can go.

Years Invested	Total Savings
10	$78,618

11

EXCHANGE–TRADED FUNDS

An exchange–traded fund (ETF), formerly known as a participation unit, is comprised of shares held in trust for the investor, and is itself a share that trades on the stock exchange. ETFs are administered by the stock exchange on which it is listed, or by a separate company hired by the exchange. Compared to mutual funds and individual shares, ETFs are tops for growth, liquidity, safety, simplicity and keeping taxes to a minimum. (Yet they remain the best–kept secret of the investment industry.) They should constitute almost 100% of your investment portfolio, regardless of your age, wealth, or financial knowledge.

> "The market – which represents the collective opinion of all investors – incorporates more information than any investor ever could know, ensuring no one can beat the market consistently."
>
> – Eugene Fama

Indexing and ETFs

To really understand ETFs, you must first understand the stock market term "index". An index is a specific group of shares that is constantly monitored for value. There are many indices that are quoted daily in the media. The most famous is the Dow Jones Industrial Average (DJIA), which was originated by Mr. Jones in 1896. He chose 12 representative corporations that traded on the New York Stock

Exchange, totalled the dollar value of one share of each, and divided this number by 12 to find the average price. The resulting number was the first "Dow Jones Industrial Average". The index number means nothing in itself, but it does provide investors with a means of judging market direction, when it is compared to itself at different times. For example, if the DJIA was at 11,500 and went to 11,615, the New York market is said to have gone up 115 points or 1%.

The DJIA was an early attempt to measure the direction of the whole New York Stock Exchange by concentrating on just 12 of its shares. Computers now make it easy for all the shares of an exchange (or even all the exchanges in one country) to be included in such calculations. This number is often referred to as the "market average".

Each ETF mirrors the shares of a particular index. Canada was the first country in the world to introduce an ETF. It was called TIPS and began trading on the TSE in the fall of 1989.

Canadian ETFs
i60 (S&P/TSE 60 Index Fund)
The S&P/TSE 60 Index consists of 60 of the largest and most liquid stocks traded on the Toronto Stock Exchange (TSE). The S&P/TSE 60 Index Selection Committee meets on a monthly basis, and is responsible for selecting those companies whose shares will be included in this index.

The following table lists the 60 companies that make up the S&P/TSE 60 Index as of July 10, 2001:

S&P/TSE 60 Index			
Symbol	Name	Symbol	Name
A	Abitibi–Consolidated Inc.	N	Inco Limited
AGU	Agrium Inc.	L	Loblaw Companies Ltd.
AC	Air Canada Inc.	MG.A	Magna International Inc.
AEC	Alberta Energy Ltd.	MFC	Manulife Financial Corporation
AL	Alcan Inc.	MDS	MDS Inc.
AXL	Anderson Exploration Ltd.	MLT	Mitel Corporation
ATY	ATI Technologies Incorporated	MOL.A	Molson Inc.
BMO	Bank of Montreal	NA	National Bank of Canada
BNS	Bank of Nova Scotia	NXY	Nexen
ABX	Barrick Gold Corporation	NRD	Noranda Inc.
BCE	BCE Inc.	NT	Nortel Networks Corporation
BVF	Biovail Corporation	NCX	Nova Chemicals Corporation
BBD.B	Bombardier Inc.	PCA	Petro–Canada
BNN.A	Brascan Corporation	PDG	Placer Dome Inc.
CAE	CAE Inc.	POT	Potash Corp. of Saskatchewan Inc.
CM	CIBC	PD	Precision Drilling Corporation
CNR	Canadian National Railway Co.	IQW	Quebecor World Inc.
CNQ	Canadian Natural Resources Ltd.	RCI.B	Rogers Communications
CP	Canadian Pacific Ltd.	RY	Royal Bank of Canada
CTR.A	Canadian Tire Corp. Ltd.	SJR.B	Shaw Communications Inc.
CLS	Celestica Inc.	SLC	Sun Life Financial
DFS	Dofasco Inc.	SU	Suncor Energy Inc.
DTC	Domtar Inc.	TLM	Talisman Energy Inc.
ENB	Enbridge Inc.	TEK.B	Teck Corporation
FL	Falconbridge Limited	T	Telus Corporation
FN	Franco–Nevada Mining Ltd.	TOC	Thomson Corporation
GOU	Gulf Canada Resources Ltd.	TD	Toronto–Dominion Bank
HBC	Hudson's Bay Company	TA	Transalta Corporation
HSE	Husky Energy Inc.	TRP	Transcanada Pipelines
IMO	Imperial Oil Ltd.	W	Westcoast Energy Inc.

The ETF called i60 holds the same shares as those just listed in the S&P/TSE 60 Index. This ETF was launched December 31, 1998 to replace two previous ETFs called TIPS and HIPS. It trades as a share on the Toronto Stock Exchange (its symbol is XIU) and is currently the most popular ETF in Canada. The Toronto Stock Exchange has hired Barclays Global Investors to handle the management of the i60s and to ensure that they always reflect the S&P/TSE 60 Index. The value of one i60 unit is one–tenth of the S&P/TSE 60 Index. At the start of 2001, this index was 520 points, so the i60 units were trading at $52. If the index were to go up

50 points to 570, the ETF would trade at $57. Therefore, if you invested in i60s and were aware of the fluctuations in the S&P/TSE 60 Index as quoted in the media, you would immediately know how your investment was doing. Similarly, you can follow other ETFs. They typically trade at $1/10^{th}$, $1/20^{th}$, or $1/100^{th}$ of their index.

The company that manages an ETF charges a fee, which is a percentage of what the unit trades for. This fee is called a management expense ratio (MER). In the case of the i60s, the annual MER is 0.17% of $52 or 8.8 cents. One twelfth of this fee is subtracted monthly from the dividend income earned by the unit. The MER is not listed separately on any statement that you receive from your broker.

i60C (S&P/TSE 60 Capped Index Fund)

The i60C (symbol XIC) is identical to i60 except that it is capped, meaning it does not permit any one corporation to account for more than 10% of its total value. (Nortel at one time accounted for 40% of i60s.) The MER for the i60C is 0.17%.

Toronto–Dominion Bank Funds

The Toronto–Dominion Bank has introduced two broad based ETFs, the TSE 300 Fund (symbol TTF) and the TSE 300 Capped Fund (symbol TCF). The TSE 300 is comprised of the 300 largest corporations listed on the TSE. Again, the capped index does not permit any one corporation to account for more than 10% of its value. The MER for both the TSE 300 and the TSE 300 Capped Fund is 0.25%.

DJ40 (Dow Jones Canada 40)

State Street Global Advisors manages a Canadian ETF called the Dow Jones Canada 40 (DJ40). Its symbol is DJF. This ETF holds shares of only 40 Canadian corporations, but they account for more than 60% of the total value of all the shares traded on the TSE. Therefore, the performance of the DJ40 is almost identical to the i60 and the TSE 300. The most interesting difference is their MER. The DJ40 has a MER of just 0.0008 or .08%. This is half to one–seventh the fee charged by the other Canadian ETFs. Currently, the DJ40 has the lowest MER fee of any ETF in the world.

The following table depicts what the DJ40 looks like when quoted in the business section of The Globe and Mail. To locate it, find the stock exchange heading "Toronto", and then look at the alphabetically listed stocks for "SSGA Dow" (State Street Global Advisors).

THE GLOBE AND MAIL •

TORONTO

365-day									Vol	P/E
high	low Stock	Sym	Div	High	Low	Close	Chg	(100s)	Yield	ratio

S-Z

25.75	13.10 SNC-La	SNC	0.28	24.20	23.70	23.75	-0.55	202	1.2	36.5
5.95	1.10 ♣ SR Tlcm	SRX	0.06	2.14	2.02	2.02	-0.08	334	3.0	
73.05	38.35 SSGA Dow	DJF	.791	42.20	41.50	41.50		124	1.9	
22.50	14.50 ♣ St Lawr	ST.A	0.50	21.25	21.20	21.25	+0.05	209	2.4	16.9
6.46	4.60 Samuel	SMT	0.12	5.10	5.00	5.00		171	2.4	18.5

Bond ETFs

There is a new and totally different type of ETF; instead of shares, it holds fixed income securities (bonds). The iG5 and iG10 hold five–year and ten–year Government of Canada bonds respectively. You can expect to earn the same interest and make the same capital gain or loss as if you held the bond itself. But when you buy or sell, you have the advantage of trading on the stock exchange instead of the more complicated dealers' market. Both the iG5 (symbol XGV) and iG10 (symbol XGX) trade on the TSE and have the same MER of 0.25%).

i500R and iIntR ETFs

On May 29, 2001 a new ETF called the iUnit S&P 500 Index RRSP Fund, or i500R for short, started trading. Its symbol is XSP and its MER is 0.30%. The interesting appeal of this ETF is that while it mirrors the performance of the American S&P 500 Index (described in detail in the next section), it counts as Canadian content for RRSP purposes.

The MSCI International Equity Index RRSP Fund (iIntR) started trading on September 11, 2001. It too will count as Canadian content for RRSP purposes. It tracks the Morgan Stanley Europe Australasia and Far East Index (EAFE). These ETFs enable you to legally hold 100% foreign content in your RRSP. It has a MER of 0.35% and trades under the symbol XIN.

To summarize, the following table lists the Canadian ETFs available at this time.

Canadian ETFs			
Based on	Acronym	Symbol	MER
Dow Jones Canada 40 Index	DJ40	DJF	0.08%
S&P/TSE 60 Index	i60	XIU	0.17%
S&P/TSE 60 Capped Index	i60C	XIC	0.17%
S&P/TSE Canadian MidCap Index	iMidCap	XMD	0.55%
S&P/TSE Canadian Energy Index	iEnergy	XEG	0.55%
S&P/TSE CDN Information Tech. Index	iIT	XIT	0.55%
S&P/TSE Canadian Gold Index	iGold	XGD	0.55%
S&P/TSE Canadian Financial Index	iFin	XFN	0.55%
TSE 300 Index	TSE 300	TTF	0.25%
TSE 300 Capped Index	TSE 300C	TCF	0.25%
S&P 500 Index	i500R	XSP	0.30%
Govt. of Canada 5 Year Bonds	iG5	XGV	0.25%
Govt. of Canada 10 Year Bonds	iG10	XGX	0.25%

U.S. Based ETFs
SPDRs (S&P 500 Index)

The most well known ETF is the Standard and Poors Depository Receipts (SPDR), which trades on the American Stock Exchange (AMEX). It was the second ETF to be introduced to the world, and started trading in the spring of 1993. It holds the same 500 shares as the ones used to calculate the S&P 500 Index. This index is not based solely on the shares of one exchange. It consists of the 500 largest and most profitable U.S. public corporations, selected to encompass all the different business sectors. Not all of the 500 corporations represent 1/500th of the index. Some are given a larger percentage (weighting). A corporation that investors begin to value more highly (as reflected by its increasing share price) is given a larger weighting. Occasionally, companies are added to or deleted from the index. Thus, the S&P 500 Index is always an up to date mirror of the 500 U.S. based companies that investors value the most. These companies account for 75% of the total worth of all U.S. based publicly traded companies. The administrators of SPDR (State Street Bank and Trust Company) replicate the index by adjusting the weighting of the corporations included in the ETF to match that of the S&P 500 index.

SPDR is one of my favourites because of its performance, broad base, low fee and liquidity. Its MER of 0.0012 (0.12%) was once the second lowest in the world. Also, SPDRs are denominated in U.S. dollars, the world's strongest currency. Because of these factors, you can feel safe holding SPDRs as a long–term investment.

Let's examine the superb track record of the S&P 500 Index. The following graph shows the rate of return for each of the past ten years. The horizontal line is the annual average earned for the entire period.

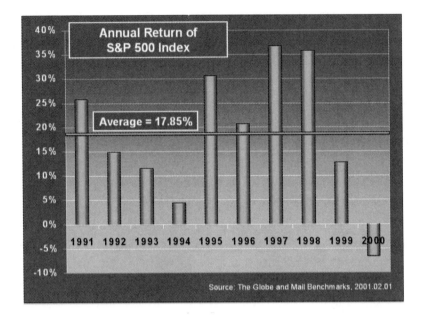

The next graph shows the results if you invested $1000 per year in SPDRs starting January 1st, 1991. The cumulative effect can be dramatic.

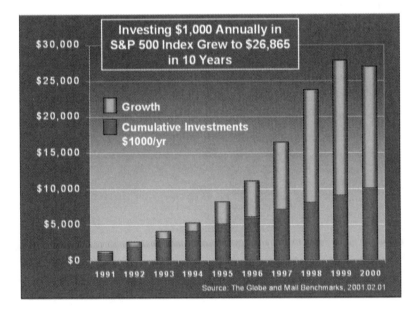

An investor may buy the complete index of 500 companies, and/or one or more of its nine sectors. A sector is a group of corporations that are in the same general business e.g. technology. Each sector has a matching ETF. For more detail, see Appendix II.

There is also another sub category of SPDRs called Mid–Cap SPDRs (Symbol MDY). This grouping excludes the 50 largest and the 50 smallest corporations of the S&P 500 index.

Other Equity Based ETFs

An ETF called DIAMONDS reflects the Dow Jones Industrial Average and consists of the 30 shares that make up this average. It trades on the American Stock Exchange (symbol DIA). Like SPDRs, its past performance has been excellent and it is also very liquid.

The Nasdaq–100 is an ETF that reflects the Nasdaq–100 Index, which includes the 100 largest corporations (by market value) that trade on the Nasdaq Stock Exchange. This exchange, noted for its high–tech companies, is volatile (e.g. up 75% in 1999 and down 37% in 2000). Many people look for the Nasdaq–100 (symbol QQQ) under the Nasdaq Stock Exchange heading, but you will not find it there. It can be found under the American Stock Exchange, where most EFTs trade.

The Global Titans Index Fund (symbol DGT on the American Stock Exchange) holds the 50 largest corporations in the world.

The 500 Index Fund (symbol FFF on the American Stock Exchange) holds the 500 corporations that make up the Fortune 500.

To summarize, the following table lists commonly known ETFs that trade on the American Stock Exchange. They would all be considered "foreign" for purposes of Canadian RRSPs.

ETFs			
Based on	**Acronym**	**Symbol**	**MER**
Dow Jones Industrial Average	DIAMONDS	DIA	0.18%
Fortune 500 Index	500 Index Fund	FFF	0.20%
Global Titans Index	Titans	DGT	0.50%
Nasdaq–100 Index	Nasdaq–100	QQQ	0.18%
S&P 500[31]	i500	IVV	0.09%
S&P 500	SPDRs	SPY	0.12%
S&P MidCap 400	MidCap SPDRs	MDY	0.20%
Select Sector SPDRs:			
Basic Industries Select Sector	Basic Industries	XLB	0.65%
Consumer Services Select Sector	Consumer Services	XLV	0.65%
Consumer Staples Select Sector	Consumer Staples	XLP	0.65%
Cyclical/Transportation Select Sector	Cyclical/Transportation	XLY	0.65%
Energy Select Sector	Energy	XLE	0.65%
Financial Services Select Sector	Financial Services	XLF	0.65%
Industrial Select Sector	Industrial	XLI	0.65%
Technology Select Sector	Technology	XLK	0.65%
Utilities Select Sector	Utilities	XLU	0.65%

Foreign ETFs

There are also iShares (formerly known as WEBS or World Equity Benchmark Shares). They are similar to ETFs, but instead reflect the stock markets of seventeen specific countries. The iShares are based on the Morgan Stanley Capital International Index (MSCI) for that country. These iShares have higher annual fees than ETFs, because they are owned privately instead of by the stock exchanges.

The following table lists commonly known iShares, and the index or the country that each reflects. They are all traded on the American Stock Exchange.

---

[31] Barclay's manages the i500. State Street Bank manages SPDR.

iShares		
Market Based on	**Acronym**	**Symbol**
Australia	MSCI Australia	EWA
Austria	MSCI Austria	EWO
Belgium	MSCI Belgium	EWK
Canada	MSCI Canada	EWC
France	MSCI France	EWQ
Germany	MSCI Germany	EWG
Hong Kong	MSCI Hong Kong	EWH
Italy	MSCI Italy	EWI
Japan	MSCI Japan	EWJ
Malaysia	MSCI Malaysia	EWM
Mexico	MSCI Mexico	EWW
Netherlands	MSCI Netherlands	EWN
Singapore	MSCI Singapore	EWS
Spain	MSCI Spain	EWP
Sweden	MSCI Sweden	EWD
Switzerland	MSCI Switzerland	EWL
United Kingdom	MSCI United Kingdom	EWU

Taxes

ETFs (except for the bond ETFs) are absolutely tops for tax planning. The only taxes you pay are on the dividends received and the capital gains that flow through to you, due to changes in weightings of companies held within the ETF. You never pay taxes on the growth of your ETFs, as long as you continue to hold them. When you decide to sell a portion of your ETF holdings, you will pay tax on the capital gain realized on the portion sold.

Summary

Perhaps you are wondering what is so great about ETFs if all they represent is the market average. The answer is that during the past ten years (1991 to 2000) the Canadian market has gone up 14.8% per year (the figure for the U.S. market is 20.8%).[32] These are stellar returns. And contrary to popular belief, it is impossible for professional investors, as a group, to beat this average.

Excellent web sites to keep up to date with the latest developments in ETFs are www.ishares.com, www.iunits.com, www.holdrs.com, www.amex.com, www.spdrindex.com and www.indexfunds.com.

Years Invested	Total Savings
11	$92,533

---

[32] Alexander Eadie, The Globe and Mail, January 10, 2001.

12

MUTUAL FUNDS

A mutual fund is the name given to a special trust, in which people pool their money for investment purposes. This money is used to buy treasury bills, bonds, mortgages and shares on behalf of the investors.

> "What's right isn't always popular, and what's popular isn't always right."
>
> – Unknown

These trusts are set up and managed by mutual fund corporations to earn a profit. The amount the corporations earn depends directly on the amount of money they manage. Therefore, there is a strong incentive to sell more funds. To do so, the corporations utilize three distinct marketing methods – independent sales agents, captive sales force, and self–marketing:

Independent agent: a marketing method whereby the mutual fund corporation pays a generous finder's fee to financial advisors and stockbrokers. Examples of companies using this method include Trimark, Templeton and BPI.

Captive sales force: when the mutual fund corporation has its own sales force. Investors Group is by far the largest corporation using this approach. Banks also use this marketing method, but most banks will also sell funds other than their own.

Self-marketing: instead of using salesmen, the mutual fund company tries to attract customers directly. The best example of this approach is Altamira, which advertises and markets its own funds.

Types of Mutual Funds

Mutual funds have been designed to appeal to all kinds of investors. All fund types listed here, with the exception of index funds, are said to be active, i.e. the managers select what investments the fund holds. Index mutual funds are called passive, because they only hold the shares of the index that they mirror.

Asset Allocation Funds: invest in cash, fixed income and shares. The manager has total discretion as to the minimum and maximum amounts that may be invested in each asset category. It is difficult to know how your funds are allocated, as it can change at any time.

Balanced Funds: invest in cash, fixed income and shares. A balanced fund is identical to an asset allocation fund, only the minimum and maximum that may be held in each asset category is usually stated in the prospectus. The manager has discretion only within these limits.

Bond Funds: invest in bonds and earn interest income. The market value of the fund increases slightly when interest rates fall and decreases when interest rates rise.

Dividend Funds: invest in preferred shares and provide investors with dividend income. The market value of the fund increases slightly when interest rates fall and decreases when interest rates rise.

Equity Mutual Funds: invest in shares of corporations. They are the most volatile of all fund types. Their primary goal is not to earn dividend income but to increase in market value.

Ethical Funds: their investments exclude corporations with questionable products, labour or business practices. For example, companies involved in the tobacco, liquor or defence industries would generally be avoided.

Global Funds: invest around the world. They invest in bonds, shares or a combination of both. Currency fluctuations affect their performance.

Index Funds: invest in all the shares that make up an index.

Labour-Sponsored Investment Funds: sponsored by a union to provide investment capital to small or medium sized businesses. They are popular because you receive a federal tax credit of 15% of the funds you invested, to a maximum credit of $750 per year. The jurisdictions of Manitoba, New Brunswick, Quebec, Ontario and the North West Territories match this tax credit, providing a total personal tax reduction of up to $1,500 per year. Nova Scotia and Saskatchewan match the federal credit, but only up to a maximum of $525. If you don't hold the fund for at least 8 years, you will be obliged to pay back the federal and provincial tax credits.

Money Market Funds: invest in short term cash investments such as treasury bills and short–term bonds. The holders earn interest, but the fund itself does not increase in market value.

Mortgage Funds: invest in mortgages with terms of less than 5 years. Investors receive interest income. There is little chance for the fund itself to increase or decrease in market value.

Real Estate Funds: invest in rental property such as apartment buildings and shopping malls. It is difficult to evaluate these funds as their market value depends upon the real estate value of the property held.

Segregated Funds: are mutual–like funds, but they are sold by the insurance industry. These funds have the unique feature of guaranteeing that if the fund loses money, the investor can get back part or all of his original investment. Naturally, you have to pay higher MER fees for this. But this guarantee only comes into effect after ten years, or if you die. These funds usually reflect a broad market index such as the S&P 500. The chance of this fund losing money over a ten–year period is therefore the same as the stock market losing money over the same period. This has never happened in recent history.[33] Why pay fees to protect yourself?

Specialty Funds: equity mutual funds that concentrate buying shares in a certain industry, geographic area or other market segment.

---

[33] The last time this happened was in the ten–year period beginning in 1929.

Fees

Regardless of the marketing method used, the corporation managing the fund always collects an annual fee or MER (often 2.5%). You may think that 2.5% does not sound like much. However, the MER is based on the current total value of your investment, not the annual income earned, which is a much smaller number. You pay this fee even when the fund loses money and goes down in value. You will not see this fee being deducted on your investment statements.

Let's assume that you buy a Canadian bond fund that earns 5% annually[34] and charges a 2% MER on your entire investment. In other words, the mutual fund company takes two–fifths (40%) of your annual investment income just for managing your funds. If you pay a 2.5% annual MER for 20 years, you will lose 50% of your original investment. Annual fees do matter.

Besides the MER, there is often a sales fee. Sixty percent of all mutual funds sold in Canada charge this fee, which is called a load.[35] If it is paid at the time you buy the fund, this sales fee is known as a front–end load. This fee is typically 3%, and you will notice it is deducted from the money that you invested. A much more common load fee is the deferred sales charge (DSC), also known as the back–end load. In fact, 82% of the funds sold with loads have a DSC.[36] It is usually 6% of the money you invested. Some funds charge a combination of both loads.

Most investors think that the DSC is charged only when they decide to sell their fund. This is not the case. As soon as you buy your fund, say $10,000, the mutual fund company pays 6% ($600) to the salesperson. This amount is immediately recorded as a debt that you owe. Nowhere is this obligation shown on the statements that the mutual fund company sends to you. But, if you decide to sell the fund during the first year, this $600 will be subtracted from the $10,000 you invested.

---

[34] 48% of the 111 Canadian bond funds (all those with a 5–year track record) earned less than 6%. Globefund.com December 31, 2000.
[35] 729 of the 1211 Canadian mutual funds (all those with a 5–year track record) had loads. Globefund.com December 31, 2000.
[36] Only 83 of the 729 funds with loads were front–end load. The balance were DSC or optional, which usually end up being DSC. Globefund.com December 31, 2000.

If you hang on to your fund, at the end of each year the mutual fund company reduces the DSC by a percentage (e.g. 0.75%) of the amount invested. In the example used, the $600 debt would be reduced by $75 (0.75% of $10,000). Eventually, the DSC goes down to zero. Many people feel they should wait until this happens before selling their mutual fund. They do not realize they are paying an annual MER of $250 (2.5% of $10,000) to save $75.

How do you know if your mutual funds have a deferred sales charge? It is difficult. But "DSC" may be included in the name of the fund on your statement. To be certain, check the prospectus or contact the mutual fund company or sales agent.

Note that the DSC fee goes back up to its starting value (e.g. 6%) whenever you switch funds. You can understand why your financial advisor may encourage you to change mutual funds from time to time.

Some mutual funds advertise that they have no loads. However, with or without loads, don't forget the mutual fund corporation is always collecting a MER. Fees can be as devastating to your investments as a lumberjack's axe is to tree seedlings.

Fees

Fund sales would plummet if investors knew the fees they were paying. These fees are so well hidden that 60% of mutual fund holders are not even aware that they are being charged.[37] The only place fees are fully disclosed is in the prospectus, a long legal document that is given to the investor, but rarely read.

Years Invested	Total Savings
12	$108,116

---

[37] Marketing Solutions Ltd, Toronto, 1997 Study (Tel: 416–366–8763.)

13

EXCHANGE–TRADED FUNDS VERSUS MUTUAL FUNDS

Make no mistake about it; ETFs are the key to your having more money. They should form the backbone of your investment portfolio. Let's examine why the relatively unknown ETFs outshine mutual funds, which are continually hyped.

> **"The difficulty in life is the choice."**
>
> – George Moore

Simplicity

At the present time, there are only a few Canadian ETFs that you can buy. Think how easy this is compared to trying to pick from the 4,000 Canadian mutual funds.[38]

ETFs are much less complicated than mutual funds. The holdings of an ETF rarely change because they are based on an index. The weighting of each corporation depends on its market value compared to the market value of the entire stock exchange. On the other hand, the choice of corporations and the weighting thereof in mutual funds is done at the discretion of each manager. As a result, the mix of shares held in a mutual fund may change at any time. Many mutual fund investors have no idea of what they really own.

---

[38] Globefund.com as of December 31, 2000.

Fees

The MER (annual fee) for DJ40 is 0.08% of the value of units held. The MER for SPDRs is 0.12%; for DIAMONDS and Nasdaq–100 it is 0.18%. These fees are negligible compared to the annual fees charged by mutual funds (often 2.5% of the value of units held) or segregated funds (often 3.5%). In other words, the MER charged by many mutual funds is 30 to 44 times the fee charged by the DJ40.

The sales fee to buy or sell an ETF through a discount broker is about $35. This cost is the same as buying or selling any other share. Remember that many mutual funds charge a DSC fee of 6%. The DSC does decrease over time, but if you sell your mutual fund within a year of buying it, you lose 6% of your entire investment.

Promotion

Obviously people working for commissions prefer to sell products for which they receive a payback. That is why mutual funds are heavily promoted while ETFs are not. A financial advisor who sells nothing but advice will give you the unbiased information you are seeking. Naturally, a fee will be charged for this service. Unfortunately this type of advisor is scarce.[39]

Taxes

ETFs are much better than mutual funds for tax purposes. First, let's compare SPDR to a passive mutual fund that mirrors the same index (S&P 500). For the entire period from 1993 to 2000, each SPDR unit distributed a total of 16 cents of capital gain income, which had to be included on the holder's tax returns. An index mutual fund tracking the same S&P 500 index distributed a total of $3.14 of taxable gain income per unit. In other words, for the "buy and hold" investor, ETFs generated only 1/20th of the taxable capital gains that a comparable mutual fund did. The main reason for this is that indexed mutual funds, unlike ETFs, must sell some of their holdings to provide cash to investors who want out. The capital gains realized when they do this are distributed to all remaining unit holders.

---

[39] Less than 1% of USA financial planners are "fee only". Consumer Reports January 1998.

Second, let's compare ETFs to active mutual funds. As already noted, ETFs rarely change their holdings. However, the average active mutual fund trades enough to turn over its complete portfolio once annually. Consequently, this type of fund generates much more capital gains.

Also, be aware that there can be hidden tax problems with mutual funds. When you buy into a fund, it could own shares that have, over several years, significantly appreciated in value. When it sells these shares, the gain is assigned to the people who hold the fund at the end of the year. Therefore, you could be responsible for the taxes on a large capital gain that was incurred when you were not a fund holder.

Performance

A useful way of understanding how well ETFs do is to look at the performance of the TSE 300, an index that Canadian ETFs closely mirror, and compare it to the performance of the Canadian equity mutual funds. *During the 10 years ending December 2000, the TSE 300 index outperformed 89% of all Canadian mutual funds.*

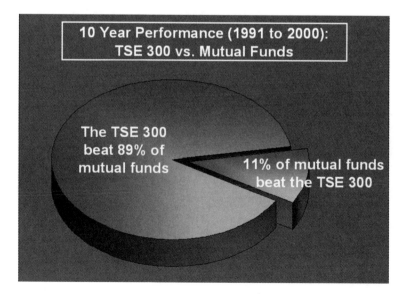

---

[40] Globefund.com. Canadian mutual funds that had existed for ten or more years were used for this statistic. There were 407 of these funds. The TSE 300 outperformed 363, or 89%, of these funds.

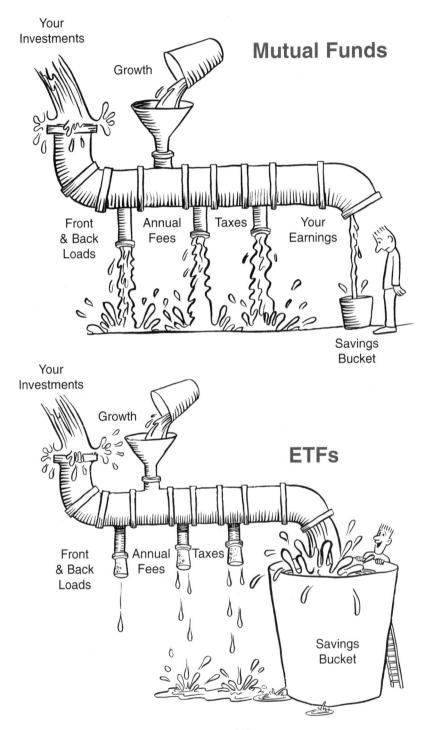

Summary

If you want more money, invest your savings in ETFs. While there are now many ETFs to choose from, you cannot go far wrong by investing in the Canadian i60s and U.S. based SPDRs.

Years Invested	Total Savings
13	$125,570

14

RISK

Many people dream about having enough money so that work becomes an option, not a necessity. The only way to achieve this goal is to save money. Then it becomes a question of choosing a risk free investment. But how does one assess risk?

Comparing the probabilities of future events is the only way to make correct choices. But this is difficult because most people are "probability blind". Psychologists Amos Tversky and Daniel Kahneman have gathered many examples of how people's personal beliefs (their own assessment of risk) are not statistically accurate. For instance, many of us fear travel by plane more than by car, although plane travel is statistically much safer. Tversky and Kahneman have concluded, "The human mind is not designed to grasp the laws of probability, even though these laws rule the universe." If the average person could logically assess risk, we would not have any lottery tickets, casinos, or any other form of public gambling. However, since gambling is a huge industry, it is evident that we want to follow our own beliefs – not the logical laws of probability.

You may be probability blind when it comes to your investments, because you confuse risk with predictability. For example, if a bank offers

> **"Fear has a far greater grasp on human action than does the impressive weight of historical evidence."**
>
> **– Dr. Jeremy Siegel**

5% interest on your cash investment, it is totally predictable how much you are going to earn, making this investment appear risk free. On the other hand, you may think of equity as being risky, because its growth is unpredictable, although it is probable that in the long run it will earn more than your cash investment.

Roger E. Alcaly, an economics professor at Columbia University, points out that shares have greatly outperformed cash investments in the past.[41] This superior performance occurred over 60% of the time if shares were held one year, 70% if held five years, 80% if held ten years, and 90% if held twenty years. The evidence clearly indicates that the longer you hold on to your investment, the greater are the odds that shares outperform cash investments. Therefore, the longer shares are held, the lower the risk.

Consider the number of years your money will be invested i.e. your investment time horizon. In his book "Stocks for the Long Run", Jeremy Siegel states that the greatest mistake investors make is to underestimate their investment time horizon. For instance, you may begin investing at age 30, and continue well into your twilight years. This means that some of your money could be invested for more than 50 years.

If you are about to retire, you may think that you cannot take any risks because your investment time horizon is very short. As a result you decide to choose cash investments. In fact, your investment time horizon could be as much as 40 years or longer. Why? First, even if you are 65 years old now, you could live for another 20 years. After you die, your children would likely inherit what is left. At that time they would probably be in their mid 60s. Once they receive your money they would probably just invest it, perhaps for another 20 years.

Assume that you have just retired at age 65. To continue living in a comfortable lifestyle, you require $1,000 per month over and above your pensions. Let's examine three different scenarios of how to handle your retirement savings.

---

[41] "Investing 101", Investor's Digest, September 11, 1998.

Scenario 1: you have $100,000 of GICs that earn 5% per year. This principal, and the interest it will earn, will last you until you are 75 years old.

Scenario 2: because you had invested in ETFs, you have accumulated $150,000. But now you feel ETFs are too risky to hold during your retirement, and instead you opt for GICs at 5%. Your money will hold out until you are 85 years old.

Scenario 3: the same as the last example, except that after retiring, you keep your savings invested in ETFs and earn 12% per year. At age 90, your savings will have grown to over a million dollars.

It would seem prudent for even retired people to keep a significant portion of their investments in equity.

The 1929 Stock Market Crash

The number one question I am asked when recommending equity as an investment option is, "Could there be another stock market crash similar to the one in 1929?" Yes, there could be. There is no guarantee that one will never occur again. This concern is a reflection of probability blindness. Not buying equity because of the 1929 crash is like someone not going on a cruise ship because the Titanic sank. The facts are that the S&P 500 Index has averaged an annual rate of return of 11% from 1926–1980.[42] This includes the year 1929. The annual rate of return after 1980 averaged about 18%. Where else could such returns have been made?

People were fanatical about investing in shares prior to the October crash. The Dow Jones Industrial Average hit its all time high on September 3, 1929. But in the thirty–four months following this, the market declined by 89%. It took fifteen years for someone who invested all his money at the peak to recover it. However, anyone who had been fully invested in the market since 1920 was still ahead after the crash.

---

[42] "Investing 101", Investor's Digest, September 11, 1998.

Since the Second World War, the longest time it has taken to recover an investment in the U.S. stock market, even if it was made at the worst possible time, was three and a half years.[43] As Dr. Siegel states, "The short term fluctuations in the market, which loom so large to investors, have little to do with the long term accumulation of wealth."

Years Invested	Total Savings
14	$145,119

---

[43] "Stocks for the Long Run", Dr. Jeremy Siegel, 1998.

15

A WORD OF CAUTION

There are three kinds of investors. The first one has little interest in investing or has no idea of what to do. In either case, she does not want to look after her own investments. Instead she hires a professional advisor. The problem with this approach is that the advice rendered is often biased because the advisor promotes the products and services that pay him the most fees. As a result, the investor often earns a sub optimal rate of return on her life savings.

> "The scars of others should teach us caution."
> – St. Jerome

This investor is often convinced that the financial advisor has done well for her and is worth the fees deducted from her investments. But does she really know? Dr. Siegel claims that it is difficult for even a statistician to judge a portfolio manager. For example, let's assume the manager annually under performs the market by a full 4%. It would require 15 years of data to ascertain if these poor results were due to lack of skill or simply chance. By that time, the investor's savings would have fallen 50% compared to ETFs.[44]

---

[44] "Stocks for the Long Run," by Dr. Jeremy Siegel, 1998.

The second kind of investor loves handling her own financial affairs. She believes that by doing research, carefully choosing stocks and correctly timing the market, she can outperform the market average. A day trader takes this concept to the extreme. While it may sound simple, trying to beat the market is difficult and very risky, as the investor is entering competitive territory.

Playing the market can be likened to a poker game; investors are betting (buying and selling shares) against each other. In order for someone to win, someone else must lose. The investor must be prepared for both scenarios.

Investors who think that they can beat the average are betting that they can read the market more successfully than others. But how realistic is this? Consider the following three factors. First, while there are 1,400 corporations listed on the TSE, just 40 of them account for over 60% of all trading. The remaining corporations are too small or too thinly traded to be significant. Therefore, attention is being focused on a relatively small number of shares. Second, there are a huge number of investors. For instance, there are about 100,000 Canadian professionals managing money for clients.[45] They are all trying to outwit each other as to the best time to buy and sell some of these 40 shares. What chance does a little guy have? Third, there is the potential to be misled by an influential player such as the president of a corporation. As he issues positive press releases, he could be dumping his shares.

Also keep in mind that fees must be paid each time you place your bet (trade). The biggest and most consistent winner in this game is therefore the Canadian investment industry. In 2000, it made $3.6 billion in profit.[46] If you have any doubt about how well the industry is doing, just look at the magnificent financial skyscrapers that grace the Toronto skyline.

The third kind of investor is someone with the knowledge and confidence to buy ETFs herself and hold on. With ETFs, she is buying the bluest of the blue chip corporations such as Microsoft, Bombardier and General Motors. Best of all, this investor is not competing against anyone.

---

[45] As of February 14, 2001, the Ontario Securities Commission has 40,000 mutual fund representatives and stockbrokers registered in Ontario. There are an estimated 100,000 in Canada.
[46] "Brokerages Report Record Profits", The Globe and Mail, March 16, 2001.

She hasn't bellied up to the poker table where others can take advantage of her. This investor will earn the average return of all the professionals, while keeping fees and taxes to a minimum.

Years Invested	Total Savings
15	$167,013

16

INCOME TAXES

Over your lifetime, you will likely spend more on taxes than anything else. It makes sense that one of the steps you should take in building your wealth is to understand taxes sufficiently to minimize this large cash outflow.

The following is intended to highlight the key points that you should know about taxes. It is not an in–depth tax course. Seek professional help from a chartered accountant or tax specialist if you need to know more. For readers who dislike numbers, bear with me. It will be worth the effort.

> "The hardest thing in the world to understand is the income tax."
>
> – Albert Einstein

Tax Basics

The personal tax return form is known as a T–1. On page one you provide basic information such as your name and address, date of birth, marital status (single, married, widowed, divorced, living common law, or separated). You also indicate if you are disabled, have any dependants, have over $100,000 of foreign property, and the date you immigrated to or emigrated from Canada, if this occurred during the past year.

The next step is to record "total income". This includes income from employment, pensions, old age security, Canada and Quebec pension payments, employment insurance payments, interest, dividends, rental income, taxable capital gains, self–employed income, RRSP and/or RRIF withdrawals, and support payments received. Worker's compensation, social assistance and net federal supplements must also be included, even though they are deducted later in the return. Receipt of these payments may reduce government payouts such as property tax credits, GST rebates, child tax benefits, old age security and employment insurance.

Now come the deductions allowed from "total income" to arrive at "net income". The most common are payments made to RRSPs and pension plans, union dues, professional dues, moving expenses (as long as they do not exceed the income earned from the new job), support payments made and interest paid to earn investment income. Childcare costs are deductible if you are a single parent and earned employment income. If you are married (or living common law), childcare costs are only deductible if both partners have employment income. Even then, the deduction is available only to the spouse earning the lower net income. This reduction usually cannot be used if one spouse has no income at all.

Workers' compensation, social security payments and net federal supplements are deducted from "net income" to arrive at "taxable income". Then the amount of taxes owing is calculated. To do this, any amount up to $30,000 of taxable income is multiplied by the marginal tax rate of 25%, income from $30,000 to $60,000 is multiplied by 40% and all amounts above $60,000 are multiplied by 50%. (To review marginal tax rates, see Chapter 6, "Registered Retirement Savings Plans".)

Using "non–refundable tax credits" may also lower taxes. In other words, you do not collect a refund; instead these credits are deducted from taxes owing. If you have no taxable income, a non–refundable tax credit, regardless of its size, will not help you. The most common non–refundable tax credits for 2001 are:

Basic personal deduction: $7,412.
Married or equivalent to married: $6,294.
Age 65 or older: $3,619.
Disability: $6,000.
Pension income: up to $1,000.

Canada Pension Plan, Quebec Pension Plan, and Employment Insurance: payments made.

Tuition fees: tuition fees paid, plus $400 per month for full time attendance ($120 for part time). A student may transfer up to $5,000 of unused credits to one other person (spouse, parent or grandparent).

Medical expenses: but only to the amount that exceeds 3% of your net income or $1,614, whichever is less.

Charitable donations: the first $200 is multiplied by the lowest marginal tax rate (25%). All donations made in excess of $200 are multiplied by the top marginal tax rate (50%), regardless of your income.

If you are eligible for any of the non–refundable tax credits, the lowest marginal tax rate is almost always used to calculate the tax savings. For instance, if you are disabled and have taxable income, the disability tax saving is 25% of $6,000 ($1,500). This differs from the taxes saved by buying an RRSP. In that case, you receive a tax deduction based on your top marginal tax rate, which may be 50%.

All income earned in a foreign country must be included in your Canadian taxable income. But you can deduct the foreign taxes you already paid (up to a certain limit) against your Canadian taxes. You end up paying the higher tax of either Canada or the foreign country on this foreign income, but not both.

Labour–sponsored mutual fund purchases generate a tax deduction of up to $750 federally, which is matched by most provinces. This deduction must be paid back if the fund is not held for at least eight years.

Tax Exemptions
Principal Residence

Certain items, such as the profit made on your principal residence, are not taxed. Profit is defined as the difference between the purchase price and the selling price. This income is tax–exempt, even if it is millions of dollars. I have seen some clients make enough from this to retire comfortably.

Capital Gains

A capital gain is the difference between what you paid for an item and what you sold it for. Investors realize capital gains (or losses) when they sell shares or exchange–traded funds.

Only 50% of capital gains are taxed, leaving the other 50% tax–free. If you receive $1,000 as a capital gain, you will only be taxed on $500 of it. This is a substantial benefit. If you instead earned $1,000 of interest income, you would have to pay taxes on the full amount. Convert your cash investments such as a term deposits into exchange–traded funds, and you will receive this huge tax break, as well as the probability of a higher return.

If you have mutual funds, be sure to track all capital gains as this will save you tax dollars. For example, if you bought a mutual fund for $10,000 (cost base) and years later sold it for $15,000, you would have made a $5,000 capital gain. In the meantime, you received T–3 slips over the years and paid taxes on capital gains realized by the fund. Let's assume the T–3 slips totalled $1,000. The amount of the taxable gain that should be reported when you sell your fund is $4,000, not $5,000.

Tax–Deferred Items

The next best thing to not paying taxes is to delay their payment (defer taxes). The longer you can defer them, the better. This is a good idea for two reasons. First, you can use this deferred tax money to earn investment income. Second, taxation of the income can be delayed until your marginal tax rate is lower e.g. when you are retired.

For the average person, shares provide the best vehicle to accomplish this feat. With cash investments, tax must be paid annually on the interest, whereas taxes are only paid on capital gains at the time the shares are sold. Next to RRSPs, this is probably the biggest tax break available to Canadians. Let's look at an actual example.

Suppose that you have a $100,000 term deposit invested at 5% interest, and that you are taxed at the top marginal rate. The tax bite of 50% on the $5,000 interest earned each year would be $2,500, leaving you with $2,500.

Now instead of this $100,000 being on deposit at a bank, let's assume that you bought $100,000 worth of ETFs (2,000 i60 shares at $50 each). If, during the past year, the shares went up to $56, your 2000 shares would now be worth $112,000. However, you won't owe any taxes until the shares are sold. The tax to be paid will be determined by your income at that time. Most likely you will sell the shares during your retirement, which is when your income is lowest. Even then, it would be prudent to sell only the amount of shares necessary to give you the cash you need at the time.

Continuing with this example, suppose you need $2,500 cash. You sell 45 shares at $56 per share, which is $2,520. The capital gain included in the $2,520 you take out is $270 (45 shares times $6 gain per share). As mentioned previously in "Tax Exemptions", only 50% of this $270 (or $135) is included as taxable income. The maximum taxes owing are $67 (50% of $135), which will be paid in April when you file your tax return. Don't forget you still have 1,955 i60 shares at $56 each, worth a total of $109,480. Contrast this with the term deposit. You would have generated $5,000 in cash. But you would have paid $2,500 in taxes instead of $67, and would still have only $100,000 left.

We have just touched on some important points. Yes, shares do not always go up by 12% every year. However, the chance for them to increase is there. There is no chance for a term deposit to increase. Even if the exchange-traded funds make only modest gains, the key point is that the tax act treats capital gains more favourably than interest in two ways. The first is that the tax on capital gains is less than the tax on interest. The second is that interest income is taxed immediately, while capital gains are never taxed until the shares are sold. The example illustrates tax savings for just one year. The longer the time frame, the more you benefit by deferring taxes.

Income Splitting

Income splitting is an important strategy in tax planning. Imagine a family where a husband and wife have a combined income of $60,000. If only one person earned this income, the income taxes owing are $16,075.[47]

---

[47] Tax on first $30,000 is 25% or $7,500. Tax on next $30,000 is 40% or $12,000. Non–refundable tax credits are: Basic personal $7,400 + married $6,300 = $13,700 at 25% = $3,425. Total tax is $16,075 ($7,500 + $12,000 – $3,425).

But if each person earned $30,000 instead of one earning $60,000 and the other nothing, their combined tax bill would be only $11,300.[48] This is a tax saving of $4,775. The couple on one income is paying 42% more taxes than the couple with two incomes. The one–income family would have to earn $9,550 more than the two–income family to have the same after–tax income. That is a lot of money.

There are two areas where income splitting can be used effectively. The first is available for the self–employed. If you and your spouse operate a business, make it a partnership instead of a sole proprietorship. This way you can split the business income between you. If your business is incorporated, you and your spouse as well as your children may take out a salary as long as you are all actively involved with the business.

There is a second opportunity to income split. Investments outside an RRSP should be in the name of the spouse with the lowest income. This method permits investment income to be earned and taxed in the hands of the person with the lowest marginal tax rate. This saves taxes.

However, for investments inside RRSPs, the spouse earning the highest income should buy his or her maximum before the other spouse buys any. As already discussed in Chapter 6, by planning and using the "spousal" RRSP option, you and your spouse can have equal incomes on retirement. From a tax planning point of view, this is as good as it gets.

Financial papers make much of the opportunity to split investment income. However, it is even better if a couple avoids earning interest income altogether. They can accomplish this by having all of their investments in exchange-traded units. This way they get the benefit of appreciating value, without having to pay an annual tax on their increase in wealth. They defer paying taxes until they need the money and sell some of their ETFs.

Canada Pension Plan benefits offer another opportunity to split income, with the full blessing of the tax department. If both spouses are over the age of 60, up to half the CPP benefit that one spouse receives may be assigned to the other spouse, so that the total CPP income received is

---

[48] Each person owes: $30,000 at 25% or $7,500, less the non–refundable tax credit of $7,400 at 25% or $1,850. Total tax owning per person is $7,500 – $1,850 = $5,650. As a couple they owe $11,300.

split equally between the two. Attribution rules (tax laws designed to prevent income splitting) do not apply to the assignment of CPP benefits. It is hard to go wrong by taking advantage of this generous offer by the tax department.

Company pensions usually cannot be shared or split. However, most companies allow a continuity option. As mentioned in "Your Goal" in Chapter 3, "The Basics", the retiring person takes a slightly lower pension from the start of retirement, but at his death, his pension continues to be paid to his spouse. Without the continuation option, the pension would terminate at the death of the pensioner, without any provision for his partner. Most people should seriously consider the continuation option. It provides more financial security to the partner without the pension.

Claw Backs

The annual Old Age Security (OAS) for people over 65 is $5,080. If you earn more than $53,960, then 15% of any amount above this is clawed back, up to a maximum of the amount of OAS received.[49] It works out that all OAS is clawed back if you earn $87,826 or more.

Income splitting has a great impact with respect to claw backs. If two people earn $50,000 each, there is no claw back on the OAS received. If one spouse earns $70,000 and the other $30,000, the spouse with the $70,000 income is subject to a claw back. Let's look at the figures. The amount of income in excess of the base amount is $16,040 ($70,000 – $53,960). The OAS claw back is 15% of $16,040 or $2,406. That is a lot of extra taxes to pay. That's why it is important to arrange your affairs so that the tax bite is minimized.

Employment insurance (EI) is also subject to claw back. If you received EI, 30% of your net income above $48,750 is clawed back, up to a maximum of the EI received. For example, assume you lost your job, but with the salary earned while employed, as well as EI and investment income, you had a net income for tax purposes of $58,750. Because this figure is $10,000 above the limit, you must pay back 30% of it or $3,000.

---

[49] Based on 2000 Income Tax Data

Note that by avoiding interest income (using exchange–traded funds instead of cash investments) claw backs can be reduced.

There are other instances when an unemployed person may have enough income to be subject to claw back e.g. receiving a severance package, inheriting RRSPs from a deceased spouse or realizing a capital gain.

Corporate Taxes

There is a substantial tax break available to people who are able to incorporate. The corporate tax rate, especially for small Canadian owned corporations, is considerably less than the personal tax rate.

Assume you run a successful business that generates an annual taxable income of $200,000. You would pay approximately $87,725 in personal income taxes. For those of you who love numbers, here is how it breaks down. On the first $7,100 of this $200,000 of income, you pay no tax. On the next $22,900, you pay taxes at the rate of 25% or $5,725. The tax rate is 40% on the next $30,000 or $12,000. The tax rate is 50% or $70,000 on the remaining $140,000. There is no way to legally avoid paying these taxes except by sheltering some of this income through RRSPs.

Now let's look at how much tax you would pay if you "incorporated" this business. A corporation is a concept whereby your business becomes a legal person in the eyes of the taxman. (It costs about $1,000 to incorporate.) The corporation files a tax return, totally separate from you the owner. The key point is that now your corporation will pay tax on this income, not you. The corporation pays a flat rate of only 22% on the first $200,000 of income each year. Using the previous example, the taxes owing would drop from $87,725 to $44,000.

Should you require a salary to live on, your corporation can pay you one. This salary is considered to be an expense to the corporation, thus lowering its income and therefore its tax. However, this salary would now be taxable to you the individual.

If you own the corporation, you are a shareholder. Therefore, you may also obtain money from your corporation by having it pay you a dividend (a pay out of a corporation's earnings to its shareholders). For the individual, these dividends are taxed at a lower rate than is salary. However, dividends (unlike salary) are not a deductible expense for the corporation.

Therefore, once you combine the taxes you pay as an individual with those paid by your corporation, there is little overall advantage to paying dividends instead of salary.

The tax advantage of incorporating exists only if earnings are left in the corporation. If the owner takes out all the earnings e.g. for living expenses, then the corporation will have zero income. All earnings taken out of a corporation by the owner are taxed as salary. He is back to where he was before he incorporated.

The corporation can make the same investments as can an individual. Due to the corporation's lower tax rate, a lot more money is left to invest. This is another opportunity to grow your money.

Super Exemption

There is a really huge tax break that the accounting industry fondly refers to as "the super exemption." If you own a corporation or a farm, you may sell it for up to $500,000 more than you paid for it and not pay any income tax.[50] If your spouse owns half with you, then together you can make a million–dollar gain tax–free! Certain rules apply. To be on the safe side, discuss it with your accountant.

Years Invested	Total Savings
16	$191,535

---

[50] The corporation must be a Canadian controlled private corporation engaged in active business. There may be an alternative minimum tax payable. However, this tax is refundable in future years.

17

INSURANCE

Insurance is based on the premise that we will accept a small immediate loss (the premium) to protect ourselves against a potential larger loss (the peril).

There are three basic insurance categories – life, disability and casualty. Life insurance pays money to your estate if you die. Disability insurance provides you with some money if you are no longer able to earn all, or a portion of, your income. Casualty insurance pays for any loss or damage done to your property e.g. your house and automobile.

Why should you spend money to buy insurance? You do so to protect yourself from a big financial hit, especially if this would cause a lot of hardship. When should you not have insurance? When there is nothing to protect, or when you can afford to take the financial hit.

Life Insurance

If you are the sole breadwinner for a family, have two young children at home, are not independently wealthy, and do not have term life insurance, then you are likely making a mistake. There is a definite need for life insurance in many situations. However, as mentioned before, do not purchase whole life or universal life insurance, as both mix insurance with investing. There are better methods to grow your money.

Buy only term insurance i.e. a policy that is not linked to investing, and only the amount you need. Also, shop around to compare your cost. I was recently mailed a fancy brochure, promoting great life insurance rates. It advertised a cost of only $119 annually for $100,000 of coverage (male non–smoker under 35). I can get the same $100,000 coverage through the Chartered Accountants of Ontario for $72. The advertised "great deal" cost 65% more. Life insurance advertised in magazines can cost up to 100 times more.

Keep in mind that once you purchase an insurance policy, you will not likely review it regularly. Therefore, not only is it important to get the best price you can for the insurance, you should also make sure that you choose the correct policy. Let's look at some areas where your life insurance needs should be examined.

Life insurance does not make a lot of sense if you are a single person with no dependants. You are paying to get something only if you die. I know of a young single woman who was paying $480 annually in life insurance premiums. (Her mother and grandmother had each taken out a policy on her as well.) It would have been much better if the money used for insurance had been used to pay down her student loan.

It also makes no sense to insure a child. If the child dies, there is no income lost, as in the case of the family breadwinner. The deceased child does not benefit from the insurance payoff. If the child lives, the premiums are wasted. This child would be much better off if the money was invested in trust for her.

Upon the death of a taxpayer with money in a RRIF and no surviving spouse, the entire balance left in this account becomes taxable income. For example, the estate of someone with $200,000 left in a RRIF will pay about $100,000 (50% of $200,000). This tax cannot be avoided. The more that is left in the RRIF, the bigger the tax payment. Life insurance companies see this as a great opportunity to sell policies to cover the cost of taxes. However, these policies are not necessary. First, there is no financial risk to be covered. The estate is simply paying taxes that have been deferred for a long time. Second, the estate would have been worth more, if the money used to pay for insurance had instead been invested in ETFs.

Banks are eager to sell loan life insurance to anyone who takes out a loan or mortgage. If you die, the balance of the loan is paid off. Loan insurance provides the bank with a guaranteed loan payment if the policyholder dies, and if the policyholder lives, the bank pockets the profits from the premiums. It is great for their business. However, consider that when you take out a loan to buy an asset (and remember that you should not take out a loan to "buy" an expense such as a holiday), you do not incur added risk. You still have the asset, which can be sold to pay off the loan. Therefore, there is no need for insurance.

How does the cost of loan life insurance compare to that of term life insurance? One bank charges $216 annually for $100,000 of loan life insurance for someone under 35 years old. This is 300% more than the $72 discussed earlier for the same coverage with term life insurance.

Accidental insurance is life insurance that pays out only if the insured dies in an accident e.g. a plane crash. All things considered, accidental insurance is probably the most expensive insurance you can buy and is not really necessary. The odds of accidental death are very low. Make sure that you are insured for all types of death, not just accidental death.

Disability Insurance

Disability insurance is frequently a standard benefit to employees of medium and large companies. However, most self–employed people, or those working for small companies, do not have this coverage. The reason for this is that the premiums for this coverage are substantial. However, the need is there. Statistics show that the probability of a 30–year–old having a long–term disability is much higher than the probability of him dying.[51] The disabled person may require full–time care, and this can put the spouse in a precarious financial situation.

The most important feature of any disability insurance contract is the definition of "disability" i.e. when you are considered disabled for the purpose of collecting benefits. There are three common definitions of disability: "any occupation", "own occupation", and "split definition."

"Any occupation" generally means the complete inability of the insured to engage in any work whatsoever. This type of insurance provides the least protection for the consumer because it is the most difficult to collect if you become disabled. For example, if you are a doctor and become so disabled that you can no longer practice medicine but are able to pump gas, you are not considered disabled.

"Own occupation" means that your disability prevents you from performing your usual work. This is the best type of disability insurance to buy, but it is expensive.

"Split definition" is a combination of the two previous types of insurance. Often only the first 24 months are covered as "own occupation" and coverage after that falls to "any occupation".

---

[51] Information supplied by Clarica office in Brockville, Ontario.

Review your disability insurance to be certain that it provides adequate coverage. Note that most policies designate a waiting period (often 6 months) before any insurance payments begin.

Casualty Insurance

People are most familiar with casualty insurance. For example, most of us have fire, theft, and third party liability insurance on our homes, apartments and vehicles. This is a good idea. Buy adequate coverage, but shop around for it. Premiums vary as much for casualty insurance as they do for life insurance.

There are several ways of saving money on casualty insurance – money that you can then use to invest. First, be careful not to over–insure. For example, do not buy collision insurance on an old vehicle. Second, consider increasing your various deductibles (the amount that you personally pay for damage before the insurance coverage kicks in).

In the casualty insurance area, it rarely pays to buy an extended warranty for an appliance. Companies want to sell this insurance because such sales are highly profitable for them. Recently, I bought a $55 electronic scheduler for my son. The sales clerk really wanted to sell me two years of extended warranty insurance for $9. This is the way I looked at it. An electronic item such as a scheduler rarely breaks down. The manufacturer already covers this product against defects for a period of three months. Buying it with my gold credit card automatically doubles the length of warranty on it for up to an additional year. If the electronic product works fine for the first six months of use, what are the chances of its breaking down within the next 18 months? The $9 of insurance is 16% of the original price. I didn't feel the cost was worth it.

The other day I picked up a video for our family to watch and was asked if I wanted to pay 25 cents for tape protection. This insurance only covers damage done to the tape by your VCR. It does not cover other accidents, such as your dog chewing up the tape. I declined tape protection, because I felt I could handle the cost of replacing a tape in the unlikely event of it being damaged. (The cost of a new tape, depending on whether it is an old or new release, varies from $9 to $100.)

An option, which can be used in place of casualty insurance, is self–insurance. This is when you put aside, perhaps in a special account, the money you would have paid in premiums. Money is available from this account when an accident occurs. It may make sense to self–insure, if you already have a sizeable net worth and/or sufficient cash flow to handle the loss. Long term, the probability is that you will be money ahead by using self–insurance, because you are not paying an insurance company to handle it. You must decide if the potential gain outweighs the risk of a large loss.

Summary

Carefully examine your insurance needs, and determine the coverage that you require. Shop around to get the best rate. Make sure that you ask for standard deductions that you can get for being a non–smoker, a senior citizen, or having no prior claims. Paying more than you should for this expense can amount to a large sum of money over time.

Years Invested	Total Savings
17	$218,999

18

ACTION PLAN

The financial data and advice available today is overwhelming. A lot of it is contradictory and confusing. Hopefully this book has helped you to make sense of it all, and has prepared you to take control of your finances. So you want more money...here's what works. Just follow these five steps in the order that they appear.

Action Plan

1. Save $6.50 a day (or more).

2. Pay down debt.

3. Buy all the RRSPs you can afford up to your maximum, and invest them in ETFs.

4. If you have money left, invest in ETFs outside your RRSP.

5. Hang on.

"The success or failure of a long range savings and investment plan is not predicated on the rate of return. Its success depends on the use of a systematic plan of putting money in and leaving it there."
– Bernard M. Baruch (internationally famous financier)

When you follow this plan, you will have a very healthy rate of return and your taxes will be minimized. In the long run, you will have enough money to retire.

There is just one caveat. You may believe that you can stay cool during a market downturn, but when it happens you may become anxious. If this is the case, shift some or all of your investments to bond ETFs (XGV or XGX). Only you can decide your own comfort level.

Action Plan Expanded

1. Growing wealth starts with saving. The number one financial problem in our society is not that people invest badly, but that they fail to save and invest in the first place.

2. There is a debate in financial planning circles about whether it is better to first pay off debt, or to buy RRSPs. It doesn't really matter which one you do first. Whether you pay an extra $1,000 off your debt, or buy a $1,000 RRSP, your financial status has improved by $1,000 because you didn't spend it.

3. In the long run, it is probable that equity investments will grow faster than interest-bearing investments. Therefore you should

invest your RRSPs in ETFs. Also buy all the foreign ETFs that you are allowed (30%), because historically foreign markets have outperformed the Canadian market. If you do not know which ETF to buy, you will not go far wrong with i60s for domestic content and SPDR for foreign content. They both represent a broad base of corporations and have a low MER.

Open up one self–administered RRSP account at a discount broker, and keep all your RRSP investments in that one spot. By simplifying your investments, you will manage them better and your rate of return will increase. An added bonus of keeping all your investments in one account is the decreased risk of any investments being misplaced.

At a discount broker, your cost for buying securities will be as low as possible. Another leak plugged. But the really big payoff is that you will be implementing your investment plan yourself, without being influenced by biased advisors who recommend that you buy their products. If you feel you need financial advice, deal with a fee–only advisor, and then go to your discount broker to place your investment.

4. Once you have completed the steps of paying off debt and buying your maximum RRSPs, you can invest any additional savings in ETFs. To do this, open up a second account (non–RRSP) at your discount broker. As there are no foreign content limitations here, you may put as much as you feel comfortable with in foreign ETFs.

5. You now have the knowledge to implement an excellent, yet simple, investment strategy. The hard part is to actually do it, and then hang on. The only time you should sell your ETFs is when you need the money. At that point, sell just the amount to supply the cash you require and keep the rest invested.

Events such as the terrorist attacks on September 11, 2001 can dramatically affect stock values. It is not easy to watch the market fluctuate, especially if your investments go down in value. You will be tempted to react and deviate from the strategy. But be patient. The seedlings have been planted. Now let these investments grow.

Exchange-Traded Funds

Years Invested	Total Savings
18	$249,759

19

FOLLOW THROUGH

You now know exactly what to do to have more money. Save $6.50 per day, buy an RRSP in order to significantly increase your savings, and invest in ETFs. This strategy eliminates your need to monitor your investments on a day–to–day basis. Not only does this system work, but also your rate of return over time should exceed almost everyone's, including those of the professional money managers. Does this sound too good to be true? Well, it isn't.

> "What a mind of man can conceive and believe, it can achieve."
> – Napoleon Hill

But the big question is whether or not you are going to follow through with this system. What is stopping you from starting right now and continuing for your lifetime? Please pause a moment to consider this.

Can you envision yourself as someone who is not dependent on a job? If you cannot, then financial freedom may always elude you. You have to know that your actions today can influence your wealth tomorrow. However, being able to see yourself as wealthy, and feeling confident that you can get there, is still not sufficient. Consistent, meaningful action must follow any plan in order to get results.

We are all familiar with the lack of follow–through in various areas of our lives. David Maister, author of "True Professionalism", writes about one example. He points out that the vast majority of us who want to lose weight have great difficulty maintaining a diet and fitness program. We understand and accept the benefits that will come to us from eating and exercising properly. We also know exactly how to get there, but we have trouble following through. Even if we believe in a goal, understand its benefits, and know what to do to reach it, we are not always sufficiently motivated to change our ways.

David Maister believes that the diet analogy demonstrates that many humans are just not hard wired to do things that require sacrifice now in order to gain benefits later. But that is exactly what we must do to obtain financial freedom.

To help us minimize some of our inherent human weakness, let's take a cue from wildlife. It is believed that geese honk as they fly to encourage each other to stay in formation and keep up. Together, using the updraft from each other and the V formation, they are able to fly 71% farther. The lead goose keeps changing. And when a goose gets sick, two geese drop out of formation and follow it down to help and protect it. Similarly, we humans can benefit from group support.

An important first step in your journey to financial freedom should be to look for trusted friends who also wish to save money in a regular systematic manner. The next step is to give and get group support. Everyone benefits. It is essential to realize that most people simply will not save effectively if they try to go it alone. When a goose falls out of formation, it suddenly feels the resistance and drag of flying by itself. It quickly moves back to take advantage of the lifting power of the birds in front. We also need to be encouraged to start saving again every time we get out of step. That is why we should find friends who are headed in the same saving direction. We will be encouraged to "stay in formation" with them.

David Maister has a novel idea to help you follow through on your action plan. He suggests that you give "nagging rights" to someone close to you. Ask your spouse or best friend to nag you whenever they see you are not accomplishing your goal. This system will not work unless you truly give them permission to nag you. The payoff is that by giving someone nagging rights, you give yourself bragging rights as you accomplish your goal.

There is another important point to consider. Are you focusing your attention on the right goal? For example, let's look at how investment clubs work. As the name implies, the mandate of investment clubs is to invest. A lot of time and effort is spent on researching and discussing which investments to purchase. However, it is extremely unlikely that club members will be able to choose anything that will outperform the rate of return of an ETF such as SPDRs. Instead of trying to decide what to invest in, members' time would be better spent in encouraging each other to save. But since there is little excitement in that, I am not aware of any investment club that pursues this objective. No one wants to do the one thing that is certain to get results i.e. to consistently save money.

The investment industry as a whole is not set up to encourage your primary goal of saving. Most of the effort of financial planners is directed at helping you decide what investments to buy, as this is how they make their money. What we really need to become wealthy is to join a group called Wealth Watchers. People would meet every week, plunk their weekly savings on the "savings" scale, and record their progress on their membership cards. There would be a group session to discuss ways of saving money each week, and ways of controlling the desire to spend. Group support would be paramount, and ribbons and pins would be issued to those reaching their personal saving goal. Ultimate "lifetime" membership would mean that you would be wealthy, and ready to help other members attain wealth too. There is, in reality, no group called Wealth Watchers, but why not start one?

If you want more money, you must take action. Can you implement the strategy of saving $6.50 per day and investing this in ETFs? Can you stick with it long enough to make this thinking automatic? Certainly it is not easy, but it can be done.

Years Invested	Total Savings
19	$284,210

20

CHILDREN

Many people have a problem living within their means. Teach your children at an early age to spend less than they earn. Show them that investing can be as exciting as spending, and lead by example. There is no better financial gift that you can give them. It will last a lifetime.

> "The soul is healed by being with children."
> – Fyodor Dostoyevski

An excellent way to interest your child in investing is to buy your child shares of a company. Since your child is a minor, the shares must be bought "in trust" for him. This can be accomplished in two different ways – formal and informal inter vivos (living) trusts. A formal trust is a legal agreement.[52] I chose the simpler informal trust route i.e. I bought the shares for my children without going through the legal agreement process.

Note that the informal "in trust" account must be turned over to the child when she reaches the age of majority (18 in Ontario). This was not a concern for us, but it may be for some people.

---

[52] A trust requires the three certainties of intention, property and beneficiary. It should name the beneficiary (the person who receives the benefit – the shares), the settlor (the person who gives the shares), and the trustee (the person in charge of the trust). The trustee and the settlor should not be the same person. Also, it would be helpful if the trust document indicates that the share(s) will not revert to the settlor, and that the settlor's permission is not required to distribute the share(s) to the beneficiary (the child).

My favourite company share to buy for children is Wrigley Gum. I bought one share for each of my three sons when they were young. When the share is purchased, you will pay a brokerage fee, which will be out of proportion to the amount of the investment. That is not important. It is important to take delivery of this share, instead of having the brokerage firm hold it for you. This way Wrigley has a record of you as a shareholder. This is not the case if the brokerage firm holds the share in street name for your child. The actual share certificate, along with some forms, will be sent to you by mail. You will be asked if you wish to subscribe to the dividend reinvestment plan (DRIP). Mark the card "Yes" and return it. This means that you are allowed to buy more shares directly from the company, without paying commission. Also, dividends will be reinvested into buying more shares. But the nicest feature of subscribing to Wrigley's DRIP is its educational value. Every Christmas, your child will receive a box containing twenty packs of Wrigley's gum. When your child asks who sent the gum, you have a golden opportunity to explain to him what it means to be a shareholder.

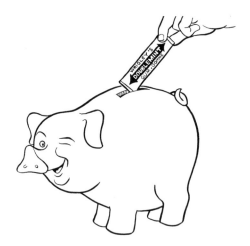

Shares for Children

The point is that your child will have experienced the rewards of investing in shares at a young age. This will have a powerful positive impact. My three boys were certainly happy to get their box of Wrigley's gum for Christmas. This "return" was very real for them, and it established their investment desire. Years later, my oldest son Chris went one step further by investing his summer earnings in Wrigley's.

Once their curiosity is aroused, take home The Globe and Mail, or another business paper, to show your children how to read the financial pages. Or you can show them how to follow the shares of their favourite companies on the Internet. Point out the current trading value of the shares that are invested for them. They may wish to monitor the share price as it goes up and down. It is their money that they are watching. There is no better opportunity to hook your children's interest in saving.

When Jon, my second–oldest child, was in grade eight, he chose to do a project on shares, bonds and mutual funds. This, in turn, sparked the interest of Kevin, his eight–year–old brother. Kevin soon became very keen on the stock market, and asked me to sell him 50 Fonorola shares. I transferred these to him from my holdings. Every night, he eagerly waited for me to come home with The Globe and Mail so that he could check his stock. He was thrilled when the price of his stock doubled. It was really rewarding to see him studying the paper and reading the financial pages. Sometime later, he pretended that he had purchased certain shares, and he got great delight in watching how his imaginary portfolio was doing.

Later, Kevin asked me if he should spend his money on a Game Boy, or on more Fonorola shares. I told him it was a decision that only he could make. He ended up buying some shares in an American company called Electronic Arts. This company makes most of his favourite computer games. He already realizes that there are choices available to him, and that each choice has its consequences.

Once your children are interested in investing, go to a discount broker and open a separate trust account for each child. If grandparents or others wish to invest in the child's future, have them put money into the trust account, and use it to buy more shares. Every month, the brokerage firm will send a statement. It will list the company name, number of shares owned, their cost and their current market value. The brokerage firms do all the bookkeeping for you. If your child wants to buy a share with his own savings, do so in the same account. For his own information, record how many shares he bought himself.

Post–secondary education is a major expense. It is prudent to start saving early for it. Registered Education Savings Plans (RESPs) offer help in this area. The government contributes an additional 20% to the amount you have placed in the plan up to an annual maximum of $400 per child. You may open a self administered RESP and buy ETFs within it. Unlike RRSPs, there are no foreign content limits. When funds are withdrawn for post–secondary education, the interest and income earned by the plan is taxed in the hands of the child. There are penalties if the RESP funds are used for anything other than the child's education.

Instead of using an RESP, you could buy ETFs and place them in the child's trust account. The drawback is that the government does not add the 20%. The advantage is that if your child decides not to pursue a post secondary education, these savings may be used to assist her in starting a business or buying a house. When the ETFs are sold, the increase in value will be a capital gain, which will be taxed in the hands of the child.

However, if the funds are used for education, it is highly probable that the child won't have much income. As well, she will receive a tax deduction for tuition. Therefore, she will likely owe minimal income tax. Interest and dividends, on the other hand, are taxed in the hands of the parent who gave these funds to the child. This is another reason to like ETFs.

Years Invested	Total Savings
20	$322,795

21

DEATH AND TAXES

At death, your assets (money, real estate, investments) and liabilities (debts) make up what is known as your estate. You may be like many people who worry that when you die, taxes will take away a large portion of the money you have left. This fear is unfounded, as in Canada (unlike the U.S.) there are no specific death taxes. The only taxes owing at death

> "In this world nothing is certain but death and taxes."
> – Benjamin Franklin

are income taxes that have been deferred. There also may be probate fees, which are discussed later. It is important to understand the tax implications when you die, because it is your fear of high taxes that makes you susceptible to products and tax schemes that are not in your best interest.

Your estate trustee[53] is responsible for filing your personal tax return (known as a T–1). All your income from January 1st of that year to your date of death is included on this return. A more detailed explanation of what must be reported on this tax return follows later. Your estate trustee has the choice of filing this return any time up to the regular tax–filing deadline of April 30th of the year following your death, or six months after you die. For instance, if you died in January, your estate trustee would

---

[53] This is the person who handles your estate. The term estate trustee has now replaced the more familiar term of executor.

have up to 15 months to file, whereas if you died in December, he or she would have a maximum of six months to file.

In addition, estate tax returns (known as T–3s) should also be filed. They report the income earned from the time of your death until the assets are dispersed e.g. bank account interest and CPP death benefit. Your estate trustee can choose the length of the first T–3's reporting period, as long as it does not exceed a year. For example, if you died on July 1ˢᵗ and December 31ˢᵗ was picked as the end of the reporting period (or year–end), then the T–3 would include all income earned from July to December inclusive. Thereafter, a T–3 must be filed annually, using the same year–end, until all assets are distributed. The filing deadline is two months after the year–end date. Note that a T–3 differs from a T–1 in that it does not have any deductions for personal exemptions.

How much tax you owe at death partly depends on your marital status, which you indicate every time you file a tax return. There are six categories under the "marital status" section. If you are married, living common law, or separated, you fall under the "married rules". If you are single, widowed, or divorced, you are under the "single rules". The tax situation of each group is explained separately.

Married Rules

All assets (principal residence and its contents, cottage, investments etc.) can be transferred tax–free to the surviving spouse, providing he/she is the beneficiary of the estate. Therefore, the only taxes owing on the final T–1 are based on the income earned during the year from January 1ˢᵗ to the date of death e.g. employment, interest, or pension income.

RRSPs and RRIFs are trust accounts and therefore they always have a beneficiary. If your spouse has been chosen as your beneficiary, these accounts can be passed on tax free to him/her, provided the money is transferred directly into your spouse's RRSP/RRIF accounts. Note that if you name someone other than your spouse as your beneficiary, the total amount of your RRSP or RRIF will be added to your income and taxed on your final return.

Taxes on capital gains made on property, such as a cottage or investments, are only paid once your surviving partner (beneficiary) sells the asset or dies. The capital gain will be based on your original cost, not the value when it was transferred to your spouse. It does not matter if you held the asset in your name or jointly. In either case, your spouse inherits the asset, and the cost used to calculate the capital gain will be the same.

As mentioned earlier, your principal residence is always exempt from capital gain tax, no matter how much it has gone up in value.

Single Rules

The taxes owing on the final T–1 are based on the income earned from January 1st to the date of death, and any taxes that have been deferred until this time e.g. shares that have increased in value from their original cost and tax sheltered funds such as RRSPs and RRIFs.

The following chart summarizes the tax consequences on most assets that a single person has at the time of death. Remember that the "single person" designation also includes widows or widowers, as well as those that are divorced.

TAX RULES WHEN SINGLE PERSON DIES

ASSETS HELD	TAXES PAYABLE ON THE FINAL TAX RETURN	EXPLANATION
Cash investments	None	There is no tax on the amount that is held in these accounts. The only tax is on the interest earned from Jan. 1st to the date of death.
Equity investments	If there is any capital gain since the purchase of the equity, 50% of this gain is added to income and subject to tax.	The deceased person has never paid any tax on the increased value of the equity investments. The final T–1 tax return treats the now deceased taxpayer in the same manner as if the investments were sold at fair market value just prior to death.
RRSPs and RRIFs	The entire amount in this account (contributions and growth) is added to income and is subject to tax. (There are two exceptions to this.)	No taxes were ever paid on money in these accounts. Exceptions: RRSPs or RRIFs can be transferred tax free to a dependent minor. It must be de–registered and taxed when the minor turns eighteen. Also, these funds can be transferred to a dependent child of any age who is physically or mentally challenged.
Principal residence	None.	There are no taxes owing on the property itself, or on the capital gains made from it, no matter how much it has increased in value.
Land, cottage, or other real estate	None on the asset itself, but 50% of the capital gain made, if any, is added to income and is subject to taxes.	The deceased person has never paid any tax on the increased value of this real estate. The final tax return treats the now deceased taxpayer in the same manner as if the real estate was sold at fair market value just prior to death.
Household items	None. The exceptions are items worth $1,000 more than their cost. These items are taxed as capital gains, similar to equity investments.	Examples of items that may be taxed are antiques, coin collections etc.
Vehicles, boats, etc.	None. These items would only be taxed if they appreciated in value.	It is seldom that vehicles and boats, other than those classified as antiques, increase in value.

As indicated in the preceding table, the biggest chunk of taxes owing is on the money left in RRSPs and RRIFs, which must be taken into income. If your total income (including this RRSP money) is above $60,000, the top marginal tax rate of 50% kicks in. Don't be angry or frustrated about the amount of taxes your estate will have to pay at your death. After all, the money in your RRSP/RRIF has been held tax–free for the longest time possible. Due to the magic of compound interest (growth of investments over time), you will be leaving more money to your estate than you will if you do not use these tax shelters.

U.S. Estate Taxes

When a single Canadian dies, the estate may be subject to U.S. estate and gift tax on its "U.S. situs" property. Your estate trustee must determine the liability for U.S. estate taxes by establishing the value of the total estate, regardless of where the assets are located. Then the trustee must ascertain what parts of your total estate are U.S. situs. Included are:

- U.S. real estate
- assets of a business conducted in the U.S.
- shares of U.S. based corporations e.g. Intel, Microsoft, IBM and SPDR. (Even if the shares were bought in Canada, they are still considered by the U.S. Internal Revenue to be U.S. situs property.)
- bonds, debentures and other indebtedness of U.S. citizens
- tangible property e.g. boats, cars, jewellery and art kept in the U.S.
- U.S. pension plans, including IRAs and 401(k) plans

If the only U.S. holding is real estate, and its value is less than $625,000 U.S., there are no estate taxes payable. This exemption climbs to $1.2 million U.S. if the estate also includes U.S. shares. Therefore, most Canadians do not have anything to worry about.

But for those affected, the U.S. federal estate tax is onerous. It is based on the total value of the estate's U.S. assets at the time of death, not just their increase in value. The tax is calculated much like the Canadian marginal tax. It starts at 18% and increases to 55% of the estate's total U.S. assets. In addition to this federal tax, the state may levy its own tax.

Don't forget that there will also be U.S. and Canadian taxes on any capital gains realized.

Let's assume that an estate's worldwide assets are worth $1,500,000 U.S. dollars and the U.S. based assets are $500,000 or one-third of this total. The amount subject to U.S. estate tax will be the lower of two amounts; it will either be the amount of the U.S. based assets ($500,000) or the value of the worldwide assets minus the exemption of $1.2 million ($300,000). In this example, the estate trustee would choose the latter.

The actual amount of federal estate taxes owing on $300,000 is $87,800.[54] However, there is some tax relief available. In 2000, the maximum relief was $220,500. To calculate the credit, $220,500 is multiplied by the ratio of the estate's U.S. based assets to the total worldwide assets. In this case $220,500 times $500,000/$1,500,000 = $73,500. This credit is subtracted from the U.S. federal estate tax bill, leaving an amount owing of $14,300 ($87,800 – $73,500).

The Canada–U.S. tax treaty provides for an additional tax credit if property is left to a spouse (a common–law partner is excluded). And the U.S. estate taxes paid on a particular asset can be used to offset some Canadian capital gain taxes on the same asset.

To avoid the U.S. estate tax altogether, eliminate all of your U.S. holdings. Or give part of your assets away so that your net worth is less than $1.2 million. However, if you choose to hold U.S. assets, there are several imaginative ways to lessen or eliminate the amount of U.S. estate tax:

- hold all U.S. assets jointly with your spouse.
- use a Canadian "single purpose corporation" to hold all U.S. based investments. This eliminates the U.S. estate tax problem, as the corporation is not in the U.S. and it does not terminate when you die.
- leave your assets in a "qualified domestic trust".

---

[54] The tax is more than 18% of $300,000 because of the progressive rates.

U.S. estate tax is complicated and subject to change. If your net worth and U.S. holdings are large enough to be affected by this tax, seek professional advice from a lawyer or chartered accountant.

Years Invested	Total Savings
21	$366,010

22

ESTATE PLANNING

How can you plan your financial affairs so that when you die, your estate can be passed on efficiently, and with as little tax as possible?

Simplify Your Estate

As you grow older, you may want to consider simplifying your financial affairs while you have the energy and ability to do so. For instance, you can sell assets that are cumbersome to deal with e.g. property, especially if it is in a foreign country. Clearly, it will be much easier for your estate trustee to sell something simple like ETFs, than it will be to handle a complex transaction like selling a piece of property, especially one involving foreign tax laws. You can also give away any assets that you no longer really need, leaving less for your estate trustee to handle. For instance, if you are having trouble keeping up the cottage, give it to your son or daughter right now. You could still have full use of it, while experiencing the enjoyment it brings to your children and their families. If you have extra money or investments that you will not need for your own retirement, you can give these to them, too.

> "Say not you know another entirely, till you have divided an inheritance with him."
> – Johann Kaspar Lavater

Many people believe that there are gift taxes. This is not the case. You may give anyone any amount of money, even a million dollars cash, and neither you the giver, nor the receiver of the money, will be subject to any taxes whatsoever on the gift itself. There is also no tax on gifts of real estate or investments. However, there may be capital gain taxes payable by the giver. The tax act deems any gift to have been made at "fair market value". This is defined as the price at which a willing, unbiased vendor would sell the asset to a willing and informed purchaser. This is important for gifts such as real estate and shares of corporations. The fair market value of such gifts may be more than your original cost. If that is the case, the increase in value will trigger a capital gain when you give it away. For example, if you "gift" shares with a fair market value of $12,000, and they originally cost you $10,000, you will pay taxes on the $2,000 capital gain, which is the difference between the two values. (Even though you gave the shares as a gift, for tax purposes it is the same as if you had sold them for $12,000.) Remember, there is no tax on the gift itself, just on the capital gain.

The recipient of your gift will pay all taxes on the future capital gains or interest income earned (if any) by the asset he now owns, but not on the gift itself. If the receiver, no matter who he is, decides to sell the gift in the future, his original "cost" for tax purposes will be the fair market value at the time he received the gift from you. In this case, it would be $12,000.

There is one significant exception to this rule. If you give a gift to your spouse, you still pay the taxes on all the interest income earned. In the case of a gift to your minor child or grandchild, you pay the taxes on the interest income, but only until he or she reaches the age of majority. Thereafter, the child or grandchild is responsible for it. With regard to all future capital gains, the recipient always pays the taxes.

Let's look at how you can use this tax rule to keep the taxes paid by the family to a minimum. Assume that your income is higher than that of your spouse. You want to shift some of your taxes to her, because her marginal tax rate is lower than yours. You have $100,000 in a term deposit. Nothing will be accomplished if you transfer the ownership of the term deposit to her. You (not she) will still be taxed on the interest income. But if she cashes in the term deposit and invests the proceeds in ETFs, everything changes. There will be no taxes to be paid until she sells the ETFs.[55] At that time, she pays all the taxes on the capital gain realized. This evens out the taxes between you and her, which is exactly what you want. You can do the same thing with your children.

Now let's examine fair market value. Should the tax department ever question the fair market value you used, the responsibility of proof will usually rest with you, the giver. So, if you are gifting real estate, it is advisable to first have an appraisal done, or else record the prices that similar properties have recently sold for. If shares are being given away, the brokerage firm handling the transfer of ownership will supply all the required documentation.

The tax rules governing gifts apply no matter if the gift is given while you are alive, or through your will once you have passed away.

If you are still living in your principal residence, please note that it is not a good idea to transfer ownership of it to an adult child. It will not change your tax situation, but it will have an adverse affect on the taxes eventually paid by your son or daughter. Let me explain. A principal residence is a house or condo unit that you own and live in. The tax act allows you (or you and your spouse) to own only one principal residence at a time, but any number during your lifetime. Tax is never paid on any capital gain made on your principal residence. This applies if you sell it while you are living, if you give it away, or if it is sold as part of your estate after you pass away. If you transfer the ownership of your principal residence to your daughter while you are still using it, your house will lose its principal residence status. Your daughter would then have to pay tax on any gains made from the date she assumed ownership to the date she sold it. Why should a member of your family pay tax on something that would not otherwise generate any tax?

---

[55] ETFs may generate dividends of about 1%. The gift–giver pays the tax on these dividends.

Questionable Advice

Newspapers are full of ads warning you to do something about the onerous taxes payable at death on your RRSPs or RRIFs. Ignore all these advertisements, as they mislead you into thinking that RRSP taxes can be avoided. Remember that when a married person dies, his RRSP may be transferred tax–free to his spouse's RRSP. When a single person dies, income tax must be paid on what is left in RRSPs or RRIFs.[56] The ads are simply encouraging you to buy a universal life insurance policy, which combines insurance with investing. This is how it works. Part of the premium (the money you pay) buys your term life insurance and pays a generous fee to the sales agent. Only the remainder of your premium is invested for you. This amount, plus the interest it has earned, determines the "cash surrender value" of the policy. (Should you decide to cancel your policy, this is the only amount you would get back from your investment.) After your death, your estate trustee can use the death benefit of the life insurance, plus the cash surrender value of the policy, to pay the taxes owing on your RRSP or RRIF. But not a single dollar of taxes is avoided.

Let's look at a real case. A 67–year–old widow was sold a $1 million universal life insurance policy. The annual premium was $71,600 ($28,200 of this was for insurance and fees, and $43,400 was invested at a rate of 9.25%). The following table shows the actual figures of what she paid in premiums and the value of her investment at the end of each year (cash surrender). After ten years, the value of her investment was $714,437 ($1,563 less than she invested). In other words, she would have been $1,563 ahead if she had just stuffed her money under her mattress.

---

[56] As mentioned before, there are two exceptions. RRSPs may be passed on tax–free to a dependent minor child, or to a dependent child of any age who is physically or mentally challenged.

$1 Million Universal Life Insurance			
Year	Widow's age	Cumulative Money Used ($71,600 Annual Premiums)	Cash Surrender Value of Policy
1	67	$71,600	$46,466
2	68	$143,200	$97,231
3	69	$214,800	$152,691
4	70	$286,400	$213,281
5	71	$358,000	$279,475
6	72	$429,600	$351,793
7	73	$501,200	$430,800
8	74	$572,800	$517,115
9	75	$644,400	$611,415
10	76	$716,000	$714,437

Now let's look at how the same widow fares by handling her finances differently. Let's assume that she still pays out $71,600 per year. But this time she buys a $1 million term life insurance policy by itself. The annual premium for this is $8,085.[57] She now has $63,515 ($71,600 – $8,085) left to invest (compared to the $43,400 invested for her in the previous example). The same rate of return (9.25%) is used. The next table shows the results. After one year, this investment is worth $22,924 more ($69,390 – $46,466) than her universal life investment. By the end of the tenth year, she is ahead by $352,464 ($1,066,901 – $714,437), due in large part to lower fees paid. Naturally, a financial advisor would be reluctant to recommend this alternative, as it would not serve his best interest.

---

[57] Quote received from Laurier Life Insurance Company February 23, 2000. It includes all fees.

$1 Million Term Life Insurance/Rest Invested			
Year	Widow's age	Cumulative Money Used ($71,600 Annually)	Value of Investment
1	67	$71,600	$69,390
2	68	$143,200	$145,199
3	69	$214,800	$228,020
4	70	$286,400	$318,502
5	71	$358,000	$417,353
6	72	$429,600	$525,349
7	73	$501,200	$643,334
8	74	$572,800	$772,232
9	75	$644,400	$913,054
10	76	$716,000	$1,066,901

But is life insurance really necessary for a 67–year–old widow who has lots of money? The following table looks at the option of her simply investing $71,600 annually at 9.25% interest, instead of buying the universal life insurance. She is ahead by $31,757 ($78,223 – $46,466) at the end of year one, and $488,273 ($1,202,710 – $714,437) by the end of year ten.

No Term Insurance/ All Invested			
Year	Widow's age	Cumulative Money Used ($71,600 Annually)	Value of Investment
1	67	$71,600	$78,223
2	68	$143,200	$163,682
3	69	$214,800	$257,045
4	70	$286,400	$359,045
5	71	$358,000	$470,480
6	72	$429,600	$592,222
7	73	$501,200	$725,225
8	74	$572,800	$870,532
9	75	$644,400	$1,029,729
10	76	$716,000	$1,202,710

The widow made two common mistakes. First she thought she had a tax problem, when in fact it was non–existent. Second, she chose a biased advisor. Granted, his credentials appeared exemplary. He held an FCSI (Fellow of the Canadian Securities Institute), the highest designation of the Canadian Security industry. He was also Vice President of a securities firm and recipient of the "Advisor of the Year" award.

Notwithstanding that she lost money, her investment was not even safe. It had been placed with Confederated Life, which went under while she was making her payments to them. Fortunately for her, another insurance company picked up her contract, or she would have lost all the money she had invested.

If she had ignored all the complexities of universal life and instead simply kept her money in an ETF such as SPDR, she would have made $2 million (21% annually), instead of losing $1,563. Blissfully unaware of the facts, this widow feels that she handled her financial situation well and is full of praise for her advisor.

Have A Will

When you die, your assets will be passed on in a timely and tax–effective manner, according to your wishes, if you have a valid will. If you are over the age of majority (18 in Ontario), and have assets that you value, you should have a will.

Give careful consideration to your choice of estate trustee (executor). The estate trustee is the individual (or trust company) who will act on your behalf and carry out your wishes. It is helpful if the estate trustee is comfortable dealing with financial matters. You want someone who is trustworthy and impartial, as well as able and willing to serve when needed. It is not an easy job.

If you die without a will, the provincial courts will appoint an administrator who must abide by written rules to handle such occurrences. These rules differ from province to province. But why put your family through that? A will is not an expensive document to have prepared. I highly recommend that you see a lawyer. Think about what you want in your will before you set foot in your lawyer's office. Remain open to her suggestions, too, but be sure that you are totally comfortable with, and understand, the decisions you make.

Keep your will simple. For instance, if you are married, you could have all your assets pass to your spouse. In the event that you both die at the same time, your estate could then be divided equally among your children. The funds for younger children could be held in trust until they reach a certain age, say 21 years old.

Second marriages can make will planning more complex. You may have children from a former marriage that you want to consider. Say that you have $100,000 in your RRSP. Upon your death, you wish this amount be given to your children. But if you name your children as beneficiaries of your RRSP, the total amount will be taxed on your final return. If you are at the 50% marginal tax rate, $50,000 in taxes will be owed. Your estate is responsible for paying this tax (it does not come out of the $100,000 that has gone to your children). Your new spouse, assuming she is the beneficiary of your estate, will be left with $50,000 less. An alternative is to make your new spouse the beneficiary of your RRSP (this money will go to her tax free), and instead have her give your children $100,000 (or an agreed upon amount) of her investments (assuming she has this money outside her RRSP) at the time of your death. The only taxes she would pay are on the capital gains, if any, on these investments that she gifted to your children. As a family, you have managed to defer the payment of $50,000 of taxes.

If your wishes are complicated, it follows that you will have a complicated will. Lawyers will enjoy the professional challenge. However, this complexity may be expensive for you initially, and for your estate in the future. For instance, trusts could be set up, but annual fees will have to be paid to manage them. Don't blame the lawyers if they are simply trying to meet your needs.

When you do estate planning, it is common to give someone the "property power of attorney" in case you become incapacitated and unable to handle your own assets and business affairs. This allows the person you empowered to act and sign documents on your behalf. It can be a "restricted" power of attorney, usually meaning that it can only be used if you become mentally incapacitated. Or it can be an "unrestricted" power of attorney, meaning that it can be used at any time. Property laws fall under provincial or state jurisdiction and vary accordingly. Your power of attorney is probably not valid outside your home province. Consult an attorney for advice. Keep in mind that the power of attorney is only applicable while you're alive. Your estate trustee takes over as soon as you die.

You may also want to discuss and formalize with your lawyer a "living will". It outlines which forms of medical treatment and personal care you want or do not want to receive in case you become mentally incapacitated due to illness or accident.

Trusts

A trust arises when you transfer money (investments) to a third party to look after someone else (a beneficiary). As a matter of interest, a trust is a concept for holding assets that dates back to the middle ages.

A trust is a separate legal entity, which acts like a person in that it owes taxes on the income it earns from the money that was transferred to it. There is one notable difference that a trust has from the ordinary taxpayer. It has the option of avoiding the payment of taxes on the income earned, by passing this tax obligation to the beneficiaries. In this case, the beneficiaries will each receive T–3 slips indicating their portion of the income that the trust has earned during the past year. Beneficiaries must include this amount under taxable income on their tax return. Note that the beneficiaries may not have actually received any money in that year, because it may have been reinvested for them in the trust.

There are two broad types of trusts. The first is an "inter vivos" or "living trust", where you transfer the legal title of some of your assets while you are still alive. An example of this is the informal inter vivos trust explained in Chapter 20, "Children". An inter vivos trust is always taxed at the top marginal tax rate on all of its income. Unlike a person, the first $7,400 of taxable income is not tax–free. In spite of this high tax rate, an inter vivos trust can still be tax effective, because it can pass capital gains and interest income on to minor children.

The second type of trust is a "testamentary trust". It is created under the terms of a will, and only comes into play once you die. This trust is useful to provide money for a family member who is mentally challenged, or to provide for minors if something happens to both parents. If you are single or the surviving partner of a marriage, your investments and other assets are usually placed in a testamentary trust from the date you pass away until they are all disbursed. This trust is also used extensively in estate planning because of the way it is taxed.

The income that a testamentary trust earns is taxed at the same rate as an individual, but without the benefit of having the first $7,400 of income tax–free. In other words, it starts to pay taxes immediately at the lowest marginal tax rate of 25%. However, this can be used as a tax advantage for high–income beneficiaries. The deceased person (say the father) can, through his will, set up a testamentary trust for each of his adult children. The interest from the money he left each of them will be taxed at 25% on the first $30,000 of income, instead of a 50% marginal tax rate, which they are likely paying. This can help reduce the amount of overall taxes paid.

A simple alternative to setting up a trust is to will the money directly to the beneficiaries. They can then invest this money in ETFs. This way, there are no taxes to pay until the ETFs are sold.

Probate Fees

Banks, trust companies, holders of mortgages and individuals must be careful not to release the assets of the deceased to the wrong person. They will often only release the assets after they have received a "grant of probate". This is a court order that essentially confirms the appointment of an estate trustee. This process is called "obtaining a certificate of appointment of estate trustee" but is frequently referred to as "having the will probated".

Probate fees are not excessive. Ontario's fees are by far the highest of any province. The maximum rate in Ontario is only 1.5% of the assets that are probated. Quebec has no probate fees, and most other provinces charge a maximum rate of about one third of Ontario's. Don't get too concerned about avoiding these fees, because probate helps to ensure that the rightful heirs receive the estate's money.

RRSPs, RRIFs, or life insurance policies all must have a named beneficiary. These assets go directly to the beneficiary instead of going through the will. Therefore they are not subject to probate fees, as only items that go through the will are probated. Always name a specific person as a beneficiary. If you name your estate as your beneficiary, these funds will be lumped with your other assets and may be subject to probate.

When you die, other assets held jointly (with "right of survivorship") go directly to your survivor. You can do this with real estate, as well as bank accounts and investments. It not only saves probate fees, it makes the financial aspects of passing on assets very simple. There is nothing the survivor has to do.

If your spouse is no longer living, you can hold your assets jointly with someone else to get around paying probate fees. The property that is jointly held will not go through the will or probate. It is wise to seek legal advice if you are thinking of taking this step.

Only set up your assets jointly with someone you trust completely, such as a family member or a dear friend, as it is powerful. They have as much control as you do over your asset e.g. bank account, and it automatically goes to them upon your death. It works best if the assets are held jointly with just one or two people, as it becomes much too complex with more. It is an ideal way to deal with your estate if you have one or two children. You should nevertheless have a will as a safety net, to catch anything that may have been missed.

If you choose not to hold your assets jointly with your spouse, but prefer to have him/her as a beneficiary, there is something else to consider when drawing up your will. You may want to delay by a week the transfer of your assets to your spouse. This is to protect against double probate fees, should you both die within days of each other from injuries sustained in the same accident.

Retiring Outside Canada

You may have a dream of spending your retirement years outside Canada. There are many important factors to consider, such as: an increased distance to visit family or friends, the cost of health care, climate, political conditions, cost of living and income taxes.

If you decide to reside somewhere else, you may choose to become a Canadian "non–resident" by severing your ties with Canada. This means selling your house, cancelling your driver's licence and government medical insurance, etc. Unlike the U.S., Canadian tax laws are based on residency, not citizenship. Therefore, there is no need to give up your citizenship. You are free to return to Canada and reverse your non–resident status at any time.

There are tax implications to becoming a non–resident. You will continue to pay Canadian taxes on any employment income earned in Canada. The tax rates are the same as for a resident, but a non–resident is not allowed any personal exemptions.

Canadian company pensions, CPP, OAS, and income on any investments that you choose to retain in Canada are subject to a withholding tax (often only 15%) instead of income tax.

In the country where you now live, all income earned (interest, pensions etc.) will probably be taxed. This may include the income you have already been taxed on in Canada. The taxes you have paid in Canada, including withholding taxes, are usually deductible from taxes payable in your new country. While you are initially taxed twice, you end up paying taxes only once.

On the day you leave Canada, you are deemed to have disposed of all your assets at their fair market value, even though you may not have sold them. For instance, you may have a rental property, cottage, and investments that you continue to hold in Canada. Nevertheless, you must pay taxes on all capital gains deemed to have been realized. Note that you will not pay any taxes on the capital gain on your house, because your principal residence is tax–free.

Your RRSPs and RRIFs receive special treatment; they are not deemed to have been sold when you leave the country, and are therefore not taxed. Instead, as a non–resident you pay a withholding tax of only 25% at the time you withdraw this money. Should you use periodic payments to withdraw your RRSPs or RRIFs, and you reside in a country such as the U.S. that has a tax treaty with Canada, the withholding tax drops to only 15%. This is an absolute bargain compared to the 50% tax you would have paid if you had been forced to take the entire RRSP or RRIF into income when you left the country.

Charitable Giving

You may wish to give some of your estate to charity. The recipient charitable organization(s) and the people they serve would be most grateful. Your will should clearly state the amount of the gift and the exact name of the charity (sometimes they change names). Then about 50% of this donation can be deducted as a non–refundable tax credit against the taxes payable on your final T–1 personal tax return. There usually is a substantial amount of taxes payable on your final T–1, which reports income such as salary or pension, capital gains and the entire amount inside your RRIFs or RRSPs. If the donation tax credit cannot be fully used on your final T–1, it may be carried back and used on your tax return from the previous year.

If you simply request that 20% of your estate be given to charity, without indicating a specific name and amount, the donation is deemed to have been made by your estate. This means that the tax credit for the donation is deducted from your T–3 estate return, and not from your personal T–1 tax return. Remember that the T–3 return only reports the income earned by your assets after you die. Because this income (often just bank interest) is usually modest, there is little tax to pay. If there are no taxes payable, non–refundable tax credits are of no value. There is no provision that allows the carry back of any unused charitable tax credits from your T–3 to your final T–1.

Some people designate the proceeds of their life insurance to their favourite charity. This gift bypasses probate and can provide a substantial tax credit on your final T–1 personal return. Similarly, you can name a charity as the beneficiary of your RRSP or RRIF. The tax credit received will almost wipe out the amount of taxes due when these tax sheltered savings funds are taken into income.

The government has provided a tax break on capital gains for those who donate shares to charity, whether it is before or after they die.

Let's assume you once bought shares for $10,000 and their current value is $25,000. If you sold them (or were deemed to have sold them due to death) and were in the top tax bracket, you would pay $3,750 in taxes (half of the capital gain of $15,000 x 50% tax rate). You would end up with $21,250 ($25,000 - $3,750).

Now let's see what happens when you give these shares directly to a charity. Instead of paying tax on 50% of the capital gain, you pay tax on only 25%. Therefore, the taxes owing are half the $3,750 or $1,875. On your tax return, you will receive a charitable tax credit worth about 50% of the entire donation of $25,000.

If you are going to give to a charity, consider giving them the investment that has made the highest capital gain.

Summary

Estate planning is no different than any other aspect of financial planning. You want your assets to be safe, to rise in value, and to be tax–free as long as possible. To do this, keep your investments, including your RRSPs and RRIFs, invested primarily in ETFs. Do not buy insurance to pay for future tax bills. It will make your life more complex, and leave your estate with less money. Use joint accounts where it makes sense to do so, and have an up–to–date will.

Years Invested	Total Savings
22	$414,412

23

QUESTIONS AND ANSWERS

The following are questions that I have been asked repeatedly. Perhaps you have wondered about the same things.

1. Do you need a lot of income to become wealthy?

It is logical to assume that the more income you have, the more you can save and invest in order to become wealthy. However, this is not always the case. Some people with high incomes feel poor, and may in fact be worried about making their next mortgage payment. They have often formed the habit of spending all that they earn. Others, with much less annual income, have become wealthy.

2. I have trouble saving money. What can I do?

You are probably not aware of all the "leaks" in your "savings bucket". Step one is to develop your feedback system. Once you know where your money is being spent, find creative ways to cut back. Carefully plan all purchases, and do comparative shopping. Carry less money with you to avoid impulse buying.

Many times, the only reason that people stop spending is that they have nothing left in their bank account. Lack of money should not be the only plug to your spending.

3. What if I die young? Will I make myself miserable by saving for a future that I won't have?

Anyone can die young. Does that mean that no one should consider accomplishing a long–term goal, such as becoming a great pianist?

Don't be so caught up with saving that you make yourself miserable. Just cut back where you can.

4. I am self-employed. What is the best way to set money aside for my income taxes?

Every month, put away about 33% of what you earn in a separate bank account. Simply choose the account that pays the highest interest rate. As this money will only be held temporarily, do not be concerned about buying ETFs or other equity investments with it.

5. You have used a 12% rate of return for many of the examples in your book. Can you guarantee that I will get that rate too?

The short answer is no. I have been advising you to invest in ETFs, such as SPDRs, which have no guaranteed rate of return. However, SPDRs averaged an annual rate of return of 17.9% for the ten years ending in 2000.

6. What does "the magic of compound growth" mean?

An investor receives growth from an investment. This growth is added back to the base amount, and now the investor is earning money on the original investment plus the growth. This process keeps happening over time. Thus, growth is being earned on an ever–increasing base. At 12% annual growth, money doubles every 6 years.[58] Compound growth is powerful. To see its impact, review the last column of the table in Appendix I.

---

[58] To easily approximate how many years it takes to double an investment, divide the rate of return into 72. In the example above, 72 divided by 12 = 6 years to double your money. For a rate of return of 9%, it would take 72 divided by 9 = 8 years to double your money.

If you do not pay off credit card balances in full every month, then the magic of compound growth is working for the banks – not you. The typical rate of interest charged on credit cards is 17.5%. If you have a balance owing of $500, and you never pay anything off, then in four years you will owe the bank $1,000. Mortgages are also based on compounding interest; imagine how much you can save by paying your mortgage off early.

7. What advice would you have for one–income families?

The concepts explained in the book apply to everyone, regardless of circumstance. The philosophy is always to free yourself from the need to work by continually saving a little money and investing it wisely.

8. I am embarrassed to invest the small amount of money I have.

Try not to worry about having only a little money as you start out. The important point is that you are saving. Anyway, if you use a discount broker, all your transactions are handled over the telephone or via the Internet. The only time you will meet a person face to face is when you open the account.

Having said that, it would be best if you could accumulate about $500 prior to investing in ETFs. There is a transaction fee of about $35 every time you buy or sell, so investing this amount will make it worth your while.

9. Should I borrow to invest in the stock market?

This is a personal choice. When you borrow to invest and the market goes up, you do really well. But how would you feel if the market goes down and your loan is worth more than your investment? In this case you might be tempted to sell, even though it is much better to sell when the market is up. A market downturn is much easier to handle if you have no payments to make.

If you decide to borrow to invest, make sure you can pay back the loan in one year.

10. *What is a reverse mortgage and should I have one?*

If you are over 61, strapped for cash, but own a house or condo mortgage–free, you can get a reverse mortgage. A financial institution provides you with money in exchange for a mortgage on your property. However, you will be given much less money than your property is worth. You do not have to make any payments on this mortgage, but the amount that you owe keeps growing because of accrued interest. Upon your death, your estate must pay off this mortgage.

If you are older, have no savings, and need money, your choices are limited. Instead of a getting a reverse mortgage, consider downsizing your house or selling your house and renting. See an independent accountant if you need help in evaluating your situation.

11. *Should I lease or buy a car?*

Leasing is popular because it allows people to drive "more" vehicle than they can afford to buy. But leasing will cost more than buying, because the leasing company must charge you a fee for its service.

Some small business owners believe that leasing is advantageous, because the lease payments can be written off against business income. However, if the car is purchased, the same tax break is available by deducting interest, depreciation and expenses.

Instead of leasing or buying a new car, consider buying a used one to save money.

12. *Should I have a separate savings account for my child's education?*

It is not necessary to set up a separate account for education, but doing so may encourage you to save. RESPs are beneficial because the government contributes up to $400 per year per child. However, an advantage to saving outside an RESP is that if the money is not used for education, it can be used to help your child make a down payment on a house, start her own business, or take a vacation. The point is to always have some money squirreled away; that way you have no financial worries and you can also help your child reach her dreams.

13. If I do set up an RESP for my child's education, what should I invest it in?

My first recommendation would be to invest it all in SPDRs. They have a great track record, and they are in U.S. dollars. This helps if your child will be attending an American college. If you believe in high tech, buy the Nasdaq–100 Shares, which are also in U.S. dollars. A solid Canadian choice is the i60.

14. Would the age of my child make any difference in the types of investments that I hold in her RESP?

You should only be concerned about holding investments that, in the long run, have the least risk and the highest rate of return. Therefore, the age of your child is not important.

15. My aunt is 65 and a widow. She only has a small pension and very little savings. What can she do to secure her financial future?

Unfortunately, there is not much that can be done now. It is too late to start talking about investments, as all her money is required for her living expenses.

16. My mother is 65, a widow and has about $500,000 in term deposits. She does not really need this money, because she has enough pension money to live on. Should this money be invested differently?

She could invest most of her money in ETFs. Historically, equity investments have had a higher rate of return than cash investments. However, it is important that your mother be comfortable with her portfolio. Because she is used to interest bearing investments, she may get nervous if she switches to ETFs, and they go up or down in value.

Her children or grandchildren will likely inherit her money. If they do not spend it right away, then the length of time that this money stays invested could be significant e.g. 40 years. This would be another reason to choose ETFs.

17. If I buy an RRSP through a company plan, my employer will contribute an additional 25%. Should I take advantage of this?

By all means, put as much money as you can into this RRSP. Keep in mind that many companies limit their contribution to 1% of your salary. After that limit is reached, buy your own RRSPs.

Within the company RRSP, your holdings may be restricted to mutual funds. If this is your situation, choose the index mutual fund that has the lowest fee. This is the next best thing to owning an ETF.

In addition to RRSP plans, some corporations also help employees buy their shares. Take advantage of this too. If possible, transfer these shares to your RRSPs to get an even bigger benefit.

18. It is easy to buy RRSP mutual funds. I have money deducted from my pay, and the mutual funds are bought for me. Can I buy ETFs for my RRSP in the same way?

Yes. The first step is to open up a self–administered RRSP account. The second step is to have a portion of your pay direct deposited to this new account. This is really no change from what you have been doing. The third step is to buy ETFs with the money that is now "inside" (and keeps accumulating in) your new RRSP account. This is a matter of placing the order by phone or Internet. Transfer (do not withdraw) all your other RRSP mutual funds to this new account, sell them, and with the cash, buy ETFs.

It will cost you a brokerage fee (about $35) every time you purchase ETFs. Therefore, to save money you may wish to place a purchase order once a quarter, semi–annually, or annually.

19. I have GICs in my RRSP. When they come due, can I buy ETFs with this money?

Yes. Again you must first open a self–administered RRSP plan, because this is the only RRSP account that permits you to hold ETFs. When your GIC matures, transfer (do not withdraw) this RRSP money directly to the account you just opened. Now that your GIC money is in your self–administered account, buy ETFs.

20. If stock prices are down, is it a good time to buy ETFs?

Your question is really one about market timing. No one can accurately predict what will happen to stock prices. Simply buy ETFs whenever you have the money to do so.

21. I have heard stories about people losing all their money in the stock market. How can I protect myself?

The best way to protect yourself is to buy ETFs. They hold the shares of only the largest corporations. Even if one of the corporations fails, your investment will not be drastically affected.

22. Should I buy shares that are being solicited over the telephone?

No. The corporations that issue them often have few assets and not much active business. The shares are usually worth little or nothing, and have negligible potential value.

23. I buy and sell shares with my "play" money. What's wrong with that?

Nothing, as long as you realize that your goal in this instance is not necessarily to make money, but to have fun. Remember, though, that a secure financial future is not something to "play with".

24. You mentioned that the protection against bank failure offered by the CDIC (Canadian Deposit Insurance Corporation) is $60,000 per account per financial institution. If I have more than $60,000, how can I have my cash investments in one place and still be protected?

Purchase government bonds. Your money will automatically carry the highest guarantee in the land, that of the federal government. Governments technically cannot go bankrupt. The two Canadian bond ETFs (iG5 & iG10) are also safe as they only invest in government bonds.

25. Are financial institutions immune from failure?

No, not even financial institutions are totally secure. The following is a list of financial institutions that had to be bailed out by the CDIC after they fell on rough times: Astra Trust, Pioneer Trust, Commonwealth Trust, Security Trust, London Loan, District Trust, Fidelity Trust, Western Capital Trust, Northguard Mortgage Corporation, Northland Bank, Canadian Commercial Bank, Standard Trust, Shoppers Trust, First City Trust, Bank of Credit and Commerce International, and Saskatchewan Trust.

26. After I make money on the stock market, should I withdraw the gains and just keep the principal invested?

Why make a distinction between the original principal and the gain? To illustrate, imagine that you have a partly filled bucket of water. That is your principal. Now to this bucket add a glass of water. That is your gain. Once they are mixed, you cannot tell the difference between the water representing the principal versus that representing the gain. All the water is the same.

Similarly, money is money. All of it should be invested wisely, no matter where it came from.

27. I feel that my wealth is not real until I sell my ETFs to get cash.

In fact, neither cash nor ETFs are real, they are both just ink on paper. It is the idea of what the ink represents that we accept as important. What you are really saying is that cash is safer than ETFs. This is a case of probability blindness. Yes, your ETFs may go down in value in the short term, but in the long term you will be worth more if you stay invested in them.

28. The government taxes only 50% of capital gains but 100% of RRSP withdrawals. Should I invest outside my RRSP to save taxes?

Even though it appears that the capital gain taxation rate is a better deal, in the end RRSPs will provide you with the most money. Let's look at an example to see why. You and your identical twin have $1,000 in cash and are at a 50% marginal tax rate. By using an RRSP, you increase your investment to $2,000; your twin simply invests his $1,000. You both invest in the same ETFs and make a 12% annual return. In 6 years your money doubles, so you have $4,000 and he has $2,000. After taxes, you are left with $2,000 cash (50% x $4,000). Your twin has to pay taxes on 50% of his $1,000 capital gain. His tax bill is $250 so he is left with $1,750. You are ahead $250.

29. *How do I know if my financial affairs are in order?*

Ask yourself the following questions. Do you have:
- adequate monitoring of your investments?
- money saved for an emergency?
- a plan for your children's education?
- the correct amount of disability, life and general insurance?
- a retirement plan?
- a contingency plan in case of the early death of you or your spouse?
- a will?

If you do not have all these things in place, do something about it. Give nagging rights to your partner or friend so that you will follow through.

30. *Should I use a financial advisor?*

If you need assistance in getting your financial affairs in order, an unbiased (fee–only) advisor can be very helpful. But it may be difficult to find such a person, as most financial advisors sell products.

Your best option may be to seek out a chartered accountant.

Years Invested	Total Savings
23	$468,621

24

CONCLUSION

Years ago, a courageous young man named Terry Fox decided to run across Canada. The fact that he had an artificial leg did not deter him. He ran from St. John's, Newfoundland to Thunder Bay, Ontario before succumbing once again to cancer. This was an amazing athletic feat. He captured our hearts with his dauntless determination to achieve his goal. Terry demonstrated that it is possible to accomplish

> "Whether you think you can or whether you think you can't, you're right."
>
> – Henry Ford

almost anything once you decide you can do it. If you want more money, you must have this as a goal and the determination to stick to a plan.

Start the process by saving $6.50 per day. After a while, the magic of compound growth will help you achieve your goal. As you can see at the end of this chapter, the $6.50 a day man has managed to accumulate over half a million dollars during 24 years of saving.

There is an ancient legend that demonstrates the power of compound growth. A man named Sissa Ben Dahir invented the game of chess. For his efforts, he requested what appeared to be a modest reward. He asked that King Shirham of India pay his reward in wheat. The amount of wheat would be calculated using simple mathematics. A grain of wheat was to be placed on the first square of a chessboard. The amount placed on the next square would always double the previous square, until all sixty–four squares were filled (i.e. 2, 4, 8, 16, 32, 64, 128, 256, etc.). The King granted his wish, without realizing that the total reward would amount to four trillion bushels, the world's wheat production for two thousand years! The moral of the story is that by saving and investing sensibly, a small amount of money will grow to a huge amount over time.

Buying an RRSP immediately enables you to almost double the amount of money invested. It can be likened to moving one square ahead on the chessboard. How well your investment within the RRSP performs will determine the length of time it takes to once again double your money. The best way to move ahead is to buy ETFs.

The legend clearly demonstrates that the money generated from just the growth of your investment can eventually exceed your spending desires. At this point, financial matters will no longer be a concern. However, don't confuse wealth with happiness. The average North American is much wealthier today than even kings were in days gone by. Yet we are not always happy, and it seems reasonable to assume that our ancient ancestors were not always glum. Money in itself does not appear to solve our problems.

So you want more money? Combine your determination with the knowledge you have learned from this book. Above all, follow through with action. Start now to spend less than you earn, and invest it wisely. This will make the attainment of your goal almost inevitable.

Years Invested	Total Savings
24	$529,335

The End

GLOSSARY

Active Mutual Fund: the fund managers decide what investments to hold in the fund (see passive mutual fund).

Ask: the price for which an investor is willing to sell his/her share. Also known as "offer".

Asset: something of lasting value that a company or person owns.

Auction Market: another name for a stock exchange. It is where all bids and offers for shares are channelled to one central location where they compete against each other. See "dealer market".

Bank Reconciliation: the process of comparing your recorded bank transactions e.g. your chequebook, to the bank's records e.g. the bank statement, in order to find any discrepancies in either, and then correct them.

Beneficiary: a person named to receive the proceeds from a will, insurance policy, or trust.

Bid: the amount of money an investor is willing to pay to buy a share.

Blue Chip: any high priced stock with a good record of earnings and price stability (named after the high value blue chips of poker).

Bond: a type of debt instrument used by corporations and governments to fund their cash requirements. They are usually sold in denominations of $1,000 (their face value), have a coupon (interest rate) fixed to the face value, and a maturity date (when the interest stops and the bond can be cashed). A bond can also be cashed at any time by selling it in the bond market.

Book Value: the net worth of a corporation (shares plus retained earnings). Book value is an approximation of its break up value. In other words, if all operations ceased and assets were sold for their recorded values, the book value is the amount that would be left to distribute to the common shareholders.

Book Value Per Share: the book value of the corporation divided by the number of shares issued.

Broker: a person who is paid a fee to buy or sell shares, bonds, and other securities. This name is interchangeable with stockbroker.

Brokerage House: a corporation that specializes in buying and selling shares, bonds, and related securities. Brokers work for a brokerage house.

Canada Deposit Insurance Corporation (CDIC): protects the investor from failure of the bank or trust company where his/her money is deposited. The coverage is limited to $60,000 per investor per financial institution.

Capital Gain: the profit realized between the purchase price and the selling price of a capital asset such as a share. If a loss is realized, it is called a "capital loss".

Cash Investments: when an investor lends money in exchange for interest. Examples include savings accounts, bonds, Canada Savings Bonds, GICs, and term deposits.

Common Share: see "share".

Compound Interest: when interest is earned not only on the initial principal, but also on the accumulated interest of prior periods. Compound interest is contrasted to simple interest, which is earned on just the principal.

Corporation: a legal entity that has many of the same rights as a person. For example, it can own property, run a business, enter into contracts, hire, and pay people. It provides a way for investors to pool their money and start a business that is separate from them.

Dealer Market: there is no central location where bids and offers compete against each other. Instead the dealers buy or sell directly with their clients. See "auction market".

Death Benefit: the payment made by a life insurance company to the estate of the deceased.

Debenture: an interest–bearing bond issued by a corporation or government, often with no specific pledge of assets.

DIAMONDS: an ETF, trading on the American Stock Exchange, which reflects the Dow Jones Industrial Average. Its stock symbol is DIA.

Dividend: a distribution of a corporation's retained earnings to its shareholders.

DJ40: an ETF trading on the Toronto Stock Exchange that reflects the 40 largest shares traded on the TSE.

DSC (Deferred Sales Charge): the portion of the amount invested in a mutual fund that is paid to the sales agent.

Earnings per Share: the annual after–tax earnings of a corporation, divided by the number of shares outstanding.

Equity: another term for common shares. It is also used to describe the net worth of a business.

Estate: the assets and obligations of a deceased person.

Estate Trustee: the administrator of an estate. Replaces the more familiar term of "executor".

Exchange–Traded Fund (ETF): a basket of stocks held in trust. It reflects a stock market index, and trades like a share.

Fair Market Value: the price at which a willing, unbiased vendor will sell an asset to a willing and informed purchaser.

Guaranteed Investment Certificate (GIC): an investment requiring a minimum deposit at a fixed rate of interest for a preset term. Usually it cannot be redeemed prior to maturity, but there can be exceptions.

i60s: an ETF, trading on the Toronto Stock Exchange, which reflects the S&P/TSE 60 Index. Its stock symbol is XIU.

Index: a specific group of stocks used by investors as a market benchmark. Examples include the Dow Jones Industrial Average, S&P 500, and S&P/TSE 60.

Liability: a debt or obligation.

Liquidity: the ease of exchanging an asset for cash. All other things being equal, liquid assets (easily convertible to cash) are preferred to less liquid ones.

Market Average: a term used to describe, as a percentage, how much the average share on the exchange went up or down.

Marginal Tax Rate: the percentage of taxes paid at different income levels.

MER (Management Expense Ratio): the fee that the manager of a fund charges for managing the portfolio and operating the fund.

Money Market: the part of the financial marketplace where short–term financial obligations are bought and sold. It includes treasury bills that mature in less than three years, as well as other financial instruments, such as bonds that have less than a year left to maturity.

Mortgage: a contract specifying that certain property is pledged as security for a loan.

Mutual Fund: a trust or corporation formed to collect money from investors. Professional managers invest this pooled money on behalf of the investors.

Nasdaq–100 Shares: an ETF that mimics the Nasdaq–100 Index.

Offer: the price for which an investor is willing to sell his/her share. Also known as "ask".

Over–the–Counter Markets: facilities that provide for security transactions not conducted on organized exchanges.

Participation Unit: a basket of stocks held in trust. It reflects a stock market index, and trades like a share. It is now called an exchange–traded fund (ETF).

Passive Mutual Fund: the investments held by the fund mirror the shares in an index (see active mutual fund).

Preferred Shares: unlike common shares, preferred shares do not represent ownership of the company, do not participate in the company's earnings, and usually do not grant voting rights. They are bought for the dividends they pay.

Price/Earnings Ratio: the ratio of the share price to the earnings per share.

Primary Market: when a corporation sells new shares to investors.

Principal: the original amount of an investment or a debt. It is this value on which interest is calculated.

Principal Residence: a house or condo unit that you own and live in. The Canadian tax act allows you (or you and your spouse) to own only one principal residence at a time, but any number during your lifetime.

Rate of Return: The amount an investment increases in value during a year plus the amount of interest and/or dividends it pays, divided by the amount invested. It is also called Return on Investment (ROI).

RESP: Registered Education Savings Plan. A government sponsored plan to encourage saving for your child's education. The government contributes an additional 20% to the amount you have placed in the plan up to an annual maximum of $400 per child.

Retained Earnings: after–tax profits that are retained in the business, rather than paid out as dividends.

RRIF: Registered Retirement Income Fund. At age 69, funds from an RRSP must be transferred to a RRIF. It is similar to an RRSP, with the difference being that a specified amount of money must be withdrawn from a RRIF each year.

RRSP: Registered Retirement Savings Plan. A government sponsored plan that provides tax advantages to encourage saving for retirement. No taxes are paid on money put into the plan, or its earnings, until the funds are withdrawn.

Secondary Market: when already issued shares of a corporation are bought and sold between investors.

Securities: a general name given to all investment products. It includes bonds, treasury bills, mortgages, shares, ETFs, and mutual funds.

Share: one of the equal parts into which the ownership of a company is divided and which members of the public can buy. Also referred to as "common share or equity". See related definition "stock".

SPDRs: an ETF, trading on the American Stock Exchange, which reflects the Standard and Poors 500 Index (S&P 500). Its stock symbol is SPY.

Speculate: to buy and sell stock, real estate, etc., with the hope of making a profit from future price changes.

Stock: refers to all the issued shares of a particular corporation.

Stock Exchange: a place where shares, bonds and other securities are bought and sold.

Stock Split: an accounting transaction whereby the number of shares of a corporation is increased. For example, a 2–for–1 stock split means each share becomes two. After the split, every shareholder continues to own exactly the same proportion of the total corporation as he/she did before.

Term Deposit: similar to a GIC i.e. money is deposited in a financial institution for a period of time. Term deposits are usually not as long term as GICs.

Treasury Bill: short–term government debt, issued in denominations from $1,000 to $1,000,000. Treasury bills do not pay interest. The purchaser makes money by buying them for less then what they are worth at maturity.

Trust: a legal agreement whereby a person or organization is entrusted with the temporary management of property (including investments) for the benefit of a named person.

Universal Life Insurance: term life insurance combined with an investment. This policy is more flexible than whole life insurance.

Whole Life Insurance: term life insurance combined with an investment.

APPENDIX I

Results of Saving and Investing $6.50 per Day

The first two columns show the cumulative results of saving $6.50 per day or $2,400 per year for 40 years. The next three columns show your accumulated wealth when these savings are invested in fixed income investments, ETFs outside an RRSP, or ETFs within an RRSP. The fixed income option assumes taxes (40%) are paid on interest earned each year, and the RRSP option assumes all tax savings are invested. Fixed income earns 5% annually and ETFs earn 12%. For simplicity, it is assumed the savings are invested at the start of each year.

Results of Saving and Investing $6.50 per Day				
Year	Cumulative Savings	Fixed Income	ETFs	ETFs in RRSPs
1	$2,400	$2,472	$2,688	$4,480
2	$4,800	$5,018	$5,699	$9,498
3	$7,200	$7,651	$9,070	$15,117
4	$9,600	$10,342	$12,847	$21,411
5	$12,000	$13,124	$17,076	$28,461
6	$14,400	$15,990	$21,814	$36,356
7	$16,800	$18,942	$27,119	$45,199
8	$19,200	$21,982	$33,062	$55,103
9	$21,600	$25,113	$39,717	$66,195
10	$24,000	$28,339	$47,171	$78,618
11	$26,400	$31,661	$55,520	$92,533
12	$28,800	$35,083	$64,870	$108,116
13	$31,200	$38,607	$75,342	$125,570
14	$33,600	$42,237	$87,071	$145,119
15	$36,000	$45,977	$100,208	$167,013
16	$38,400	$49,828	$114,921	$191,535
17	$40,800	$53,795	$131,399	$218,999
18	$43,200	$57,880	$149,855	$249,759
19	$45,600	$62,089	$170,526	$284,210
20	$48,000	$66,424	$193,677	$322,795

Results of Saving and Investing $6.50 per Day			
Year	Cumulative Savings	Fixed Income	ETFs	ETFs in RRSPs
21	$50,400	$70,888	$219,606	$366,010
22	$52,800	$75,487	$248,647	$414,412
23	$55,200	$80,224	$281,173	$468,621
24	$57,600	$85,102	$317,601	$529,335
25	$60,000	$90,127	$358,401	$597,336
26	$62,400	$95,303	$404,098	$673,496
27	$64,800	$100,634	$455,277	$758,796
28	$67,200	$106,125	$512,599	$854,331
29	$69,600	$111,781	$576,798	$961,331
30	$72,000	$117,606	$648,702	$1,081,170
31	$74,400	$123,607	$729,235	$1,215,391
32	$76,800	$129,787	$819,431	$1,365,718
33	$79,200	$136,152	$920,450	$1,534,084
34	$81,600	$142,709	$1,033,592	$1,722,654
35	$84,000	$149,462	$1,160,311	$1,933,852
36	$86,400	$156,418	$1,302,237	$2,170,395
37	$88,800	$163,583	$1,461,193	$2,435,322
38	$91,200	$170,962	$1,639,224	$2,732,041
39	$93,600	$178,563	$1,838,619	$3,064,366
40	$96,000	$186,392	$2,061,942	$3,436,570

APPENDIX II

Select Sector Funds

Basic Industries Select Sector (Symbol XLB)
This unit is composed of nearly 60 companies involved in such basic industries as integrated steel products, chemicals, fibres, paper and gold. Among its largest components are Dupont, Monsanto and Dow Chemical.

Consumer Services Select Sector (Symbol XLV)
Companies in this sector of more than 40 stocks include entertainment, publishing, prepared foods, medical services, and lodging e.g. Walt Disney, Time Warner and McDonald's.

Consumer Staples Select Sector (Symbol XLP)
The companies in this sector are all involved in the development and production of consumer products that cover cosmetic and personal care, pharmaceuticals, soft drinks, tobacco and food products. Its more than 60 component stocks include Coca–Cola, Merck and Pfizer.

Cyclical/Transportation Select Sector (Symbol XLY)
Building materials, retailing, apparel, housewares, air transportation, automotive manufacturing, shipping and trucking are all represented in this group. This nearly 70–stock sector includes Wal–Mart, Ford Motor and Home Depot.

Energy Select Sector (Symbol XLE)
Energy companies in this more than 30–stock unit develop and produce crude oil and natural gas, and provide drilling and other energy–related services. Leaders in the group include Exxon, Royal Dutch Petroleum and Chevron.

Financial Select Sector (Symbol XLF)

A wide array of diversified financial service firms are featured in this sector with businesses ranging from investment management to commercial and investment banking. Among the more than 70 companies included in the unit are American International Group, Citigroup and BankAmerica.

Industrial Select Sector (Symbol XLI)

General Electric, Minnesota Mining & Manufacturing, and Tyco International are among the largest components in this more than 30-stock sector. Industries include electrical equipment, construction equipment, waste management services and industrial machinery products.

Technology Select Sector (Symbol XLK)

Nearly 80 stocks covering products developed by defence manufacturers, telecommunications equipment, microcomputer components, integrated computer circuits and process monitoring systems are included in this unit. Components include Microsoft, Intel and IBM.

Utilities Select Sector (Symbol XLU)

Utilities provide communication services, electrical power and natural gas distribution. The 39 component companies include Bell Atlantic, SBC Communications and BellSouth.

INDEX

A

B

C

D

R

S

T

U

V

W

George Caners is available as a keynote speaker or to present financial planning seminars.

For further information or to order books directly, please contact his office:

George Caners C.A.
9 Broad Street Suite 210
Brockville, Ontario
K6V 6Z4

Phone: 613–342–1555 or toll free at 888–829–9952

Email: george@caners.com

Fax: 613–342–2845

You may also visit his website at www.caners.com